pencils PAPER & prayer

Christian
Devotions
for
Educators

pencils

PAPER

&

prayer

Matt Stephen, Ed.D.

TATE PUBLISHING & *Enterprises*

Published by Tate Publishing & Enterprises, LLC
127 E. Trade Center Terrace | Mustang, Oklahoma 73064 USA
1.888.361.9473 | www.tatepublishing.com

Tate Publishing is committed to excellence in the publishing industry. The company reflects the philosophy established by the founders, based on Psalm 68:11,
"The Lord gave the word and great was the company of those who published it."

Book design copyright © 2010 by Tate Publishing, LLC. All rights reserved.
Cover design by Amber Gulilat
Interior design by Nathan Harmony

Published in the United States of America

ISBN: 978-1-61663-852-8
1. Religion: Christian Life: Devotional
2. Education: Essays
10.07.08

Dedication

This book is dedicated to God and all educators who serve his children.

Matt Stephen

Acknowledgments

I wish to thank God for his daily guidance and for blessing me with the intense desire to research and apply servant leadership to the school setting. I also thank my wife, Martha, and my family who have always provided me with their unconditional love and support. I would like to express my gratitude to all of the professional colleagues, friends, students, parents, and community members who have blessed me with the relationships and experiences that assisted me in writing these devotions. We have all provided one another with wonderful stories to tell.

Table of Contents

Introduction

Serving children in our schools is one of God's greatest callings. God put us in this world to serve one another and share his love, and we educators are in the ideal profession to carry out his will. God has placed us in a position to influence his children, and he requires that we provide them with a Christian role model. Accepting God's call can be a challenge for those of us who are serving children in the secular world of public education where it is not readily acceptable to speak of God's will.

If we desire to be Christian servant leaders (leaders who aspire to achieve God's standards), we must pass God's test for leadership. We are held to the very highest of standards regarding our attitudes and behaviors, and the pressure is on. In order to meet God's standards for servant leadership, we must examine his word and aspire to live and work within his will. We need God's guidance to overcome the daily challenges of leadership in our classrooms. God has called us to care for his children; and with his guidance, we can lead our students to their best futures!

I have thirty years of experience as an educator in public schools. I have served as a teacher, counselor, assistant principal, principal, central office administrator, and university professor. Over the years, I learned that servant leadership is not the easiest way to lead, but God never promised us that leading his children would be a simple task. During my journey from teacher to assistant superintendent, God taught me to be humble and to depend upon him for success; and joyfully, I have learned that the rewards for servant leadership are immeasurable and eternal!

The devotions in this book are based upon God's word and designed to explore the joys and challenges of Christian servant leadership in our classrooms and our schools. This book is written for educators of all levels, pre-kindergarten through post-high school. These devotions follow a traditional public school calendar and many devotions are written with the classroom teacher in mind. However, they are appropriate for all who support classroom teachers, such as administrators, campus and central office support personnel, paraprofessionals, and classified personnel. God's word and his will for Christian leadership are crucial for the success of educators who serve his children.

These devotions are set up on a month-to-month basis with topics that are relevant for the month in which they fall. I suggest that you read two or three of these devotions per week and allow yourself time to contemplate God's word and his will for you as you guide his children. God will speak to you as you read his word and commune with him, so write notes to yourself as you read these devotions. I also suggest that you be bold and meet in small groups with fellow educators to discuss these devotions and determine steps needed to promote servant leadership at your schools. I pray that God will use these devotions to speak to us, make us laugh and cry, challenge us to reflect, revive our spirits, inspire us to action, and increase the joy we receive from serving his children.

Join me in celebrating the joys and challenges of Christian servant leadership! Let's explore God's will and strengthen our relationship with him. Together, let's reflect on the greatest of callings—to serve God and his children. Let's rely upon God to help us renew our service spirits. As King David once sang:

> Create in me a clean heart, O God. Renew a right spirit within me.
>
> Psalm 51:10

Dear Father,

Thank you for putting me in the greatest position of all—to serve your children. I will pray daily to seek your guidance. Please grant me your peace, wisdom, strength, and patience so that I may follow your will and properly serve your children. Amen.

August

August always arrives sooner than expected. It is not true that we are in the education business for three reasons: June, July, and August. Neither is it true that educators have three months of paid vacation. It is true that educators have time over the summer months to do as they choose: rest and relax, go on vacation, spend time with family, work additional jobs, take college courses, take in some professional development activities, and/or plan for the next school year. I always found summer to be a mixed blessing with time off to have some fun, but very little money to help provide the fun. If teachers were paid what they deserve, cruise ships and luxury resorts would be filled with teachers all summer.

August is a month of preparation. We wrap up summer vacation and prepare for the new school year. We are busy organizing our rooms, planning curriculum scope and sequence, gathering materials, and preparing for opening day. Preparation for the new school year can be done alone or in groups. Several heads are better than one when planning for God's children, so we should utilize one another's strengths as we plan the instructional activities. Cooperative planning is a force that can turn good schools into great schools.

August is also a time for goal setting. We plan student instructional goals for classrooms, subject-areas, campuses, and even districts. We also plan goals for staff in-service and school activities for the year. This is also the time to plan goals for our personal growth. We can take time to reflect on where we are in our careers and set some goals to attain this year. We must see to our own personal and professional growth. Administrators try to help us grow professionally, but only we are aware of our true personal and professional growth needs. It is imperative that we talk to God regarding his will for us this year. His growth plan for us is the greatest development of all.

August is a time for establishing relationships. We are meeting new colleagues and new students. We have new relationships to build and previous relationships to maintain and improve. We need to make it a priority to meet all new staff members on our campuses and offer our help, and we should follow up and check on them

Matt Stephen, Ed.D.

several times throughout the next few weeks. Do you remember your first year of teaching? Wouldn't you have been grateful for someone like you to come along and offer assistance?

There is an air of excitement about beginning the new school year, and along with that excitement comes a little anxiety. Even veteran teachers can feel tension regarding the "unknowns" of a new school year. A good night's sleep can be hard to get. We can ask God to grant us his peace and preside over our sleep as we approach opening day.

A Teacher's Prayer

Dear Father,
> You are my counsel and my guide,
> the guardian and protector at my side.
> You are my hope—joy and peace you give.
> You are my purpose—my reason to live.

> I admit that sometimes I am too busy to touch,
> sometimes I think of myself too much,
> sometimes my patience runs too thin,
> sometimes my tunnel vision kicks in.

> Thank you for allowing me to serve your children well,
> for giving me intelligence and a story to tell,
> for granting me freedom of choice in what I do,
> for the eternity I get to spend with you.

> Please help my teaching to be creative and fun,
> supply me with endurance to get my job done,
> restore my sense of purpose and focus on others,
> grant me patience with my sisters and brothers.

> Most of all, I pray for my students' future.
> As your instrument, I will try to assure
> that they grow in character strong and true
> and accomplish all you plan for them to do.
> Amen.

We need to pray for ourselves and our children every day.
As Paul told us:

Matt Stephen, Ed.D.

I urge you first of all, to pray for all people. As you make your requests, plead for God's mercy upon them, and give thanks.

1 Timothy 2:1

Dear Father,

We will pray for our children daily. Thank you for our ability to make a difference for your children. With your guidance, we will lead your children within your will and raise them for your glory. Amen.

How to Love a Teacher

I loved my kindergarten teacher with a passion. She was a grandmotherly-type person who was very patient and loving. I can remember getting lots of lap time with her (could it be the lap time was really a way of holding me still?). My kindergarten teacher loved me as well. She told my mother that I had a special sense of humor that should never be taken away from me. In contrast, my first grade teacher told my mother that I was a "clown" who should put his energies into his schoolwork and not into entertaining the other students. Can one guess which of these teachers I vividly remember and continue to love to this day?

Kids love their teachers. They show their love in different ways. The little ones will unashamedly demand hugs or write love poems. I once saw a Valentine's Day card that one little first grade Romeo gave to his teacher on which he wrote, "I love you until the end of time." Our older students are a little more subtle in expressing their love and admiration. They will hang around for a few extra minutes before and after class to talk or be with us. It felt great to me as a teacher to have to shoo the students out of my room in order for them to get to their next class on time. Our students' love for us does not happen accidentally. We earn it.

King David sang in one of his psalms that we love God because he cares about us:

> I love the Lord because he hears and answers my prayers. Because he bends down and listens, I will pray as long as I have breath!
>
> Psalm 116:1–2

Matt Stephen, Ed.D.

As servant leaders in the classroom, we have the opportunity to show the same kind of love that God demonstrates for us. Just as in our relationship with our Lord, our kids love us because we listen and show them that we care.

Here are some ways we can "bend down" and listen to our children:

- Smile at them
- Stop and spend time with them
- Laugh with them
- Talk to them
- Listen to them
- Ask about them and their family
- Work with them
- Respect them; ask for their opinions
- Care about them
- Touch them
- Encourage them
- Challenge them
- Protect them
- Praise them

God takes the time to listen to us and answer our prayers. He loves us. He stops to listen. He bends down to be with us. He takes care of us. He knows us. He has counted the hairs on each of our heads.

Dear Father,

We love you because you hear and answer our prayers. Thank you for providing the perfect model for loving others. Please guide our thoughts and actions so we can show our love for others each day. Amen.

Heart vs. Stuff

Every year we pursue the perfect program, curriculum, and instructional strategy for successful student achievement. I call this the NIFTY pursuit (New Idea for This Year). Sometimes these NIFTY concepts are new, but usually they are old ideas repackaged under a new name. In my thirty years of public school service, I have accumulated a long list of NIFTY experiences: cooperative learning, mastery learning, cognitive brain theory, multiple intelligences, learning theories, learning styles, assertive discipline, cooperative discipline, social skills models, character education, interdisciplinary approaches to instruction, and curriculum alignment to name a few; and the list gets longer with each new school year. As a teacher and as an administrator, I always wondered, "What is going to be the NIFTY?"

Although new theories, strategies and materials are a helpful part of an educator's repertoire, the single most important factor determining student success has remained constant over the years—the quality of the relationship established between the teacher and the child. Simply stated, people make the difference in an organization. All of the most recent, most expensive, and most effective instructional materials and programs will make little difference if there is not a quality person to implement them. Moreover, the success of these NIFTY ideas is dependent upon the quality of the personal relationship established between teacher and student. Therefore, it is not what the schools have, but whom the schools have that make the difference for students!

God has told us that it is not what we have, but who we are and what we do that makes the difference:

> I don't need the bulls you sacrifice; I don't need the blood of goats. What I want instead is your true thanks to God; I want you to fulfill your vows to the Most High. Trust me in your times of trouble, and I will rescue you, and you will give me glory.
>
> Psalm 50:13–15

God wants our hearts, not our "stuff." So do our children. The best materials and programs are useless if the students are not motivated to learn. We must concentrate on establishing relationships and rapport with our students. Students will work harder if they like and respect their teachers. When children realize that we have dedicated our hearts to them, they will in turn give us their hearts and minds.

Dear Father,

You have our hearts because we know that you want our hearts and not our stuff. We have also given our hearts away to your children. Help us to remain ever mindful that we must daily show our students that we care for them and want the best for them. Amen.

Matt Stephen, Ed.D.

Dumber Words Were Never Spoken

I have a nomination for the dumbest words ever spoken—the old saying, "Those who can, do; those who can't, teach." I would like to know which genius dreamed up this foolish statement because I have some things to say to him or her. This statement makes teachers sound like losers. It is true that anyone can teach. In fact, all of us have taught something to someone at some point. Most adults have taught a child to tie a shoe or ride a bike. The fallacy here is that these personal teaching experiences give many people the idea that they are qualified to instruct schoolteachers on how to teach in the classroom. Although anyone can teach another person a certain skill or content, the art of teaching is not a task at which everyone can succeed.

Mastering the art of teaching is difficult. First, teachers work daily with a room full of students who are at different levels of ability and motivation. For each subject, teachers must begin by assessing what each student knows. Then teachers determine not only what students need to learn but also how each one learns best. Teachers individualize learning experiences and make them interesting and relevant to the students' lives. Teachers must then enable the students to understand why learning is important and motivate them to want to do their best to learn all they can. In addition to all of this, teachers are called upon to act as counselors, judges, entertainers, stage directors, negotiators, and politicians. Sound easy? Maybe we should let our critics take a shot at it!

Educators are victims of criticism and sarcasm; however, we are the bedrock of our society. We are not the flashy heroes or superstars that the children most admire, but we are the solid rock upon which they depend to help them construct their best future. We may not be regarded as celebrities by society, but we are the ones that keep our country moving forward. Educators deserve enthusiastic cheers and accolades. Society should put them up on a pedestal for what they do! We should see educators on magazine covers, trading cards, and television commercials!

Although educators deserve countless accolades, Jesus tells us that our deeds are not to be done for the public's admiration:

> Take care! Don't do your good deeds publicly, to be admired, because then you will lose the reward from your Father in heaven.
>
> Matthew 6:1

We are told not to seek admiration or applause for what we do. If we did, our focus would be on ourselves, not on God and his children. We are working for our Father in heaven. He promises us that our reward is waiting for us. Once in heaven, we will most likely wonder why we were more concerned with human praise than in pleasing God. We will understand that accolades from anyone other than God are trivial.

Dear Father,

We thank you for the privilege of serving you and your children. We know that our reward is eternal life with you. Our work here is important, but it is not often recognized as such. Help us to weather the criticisms and give us the strength to do our best. Amen.

September

September is a month of new beginnings and new opportunities. We are building new relationships with our students. We can immediately get to know each child with whom we are working. We can involve ourselves in personal conversations with each child whenever possible to learn who they truly are. It is important that we smile and demonstrate genuine concern for students beginning the first minute we meet them. We make it a priority to identify special needs of students right away, even if it requires seeking help from other people to gain information or knowledge about a child.

We are also building relationships with our colleagues. We may already know most of our co-workers, but there is always someone we need to get to know better. Our schools are filled with people who serve kids: custodians, food service employees, secretaries, teacher assistants, and auxiliary personnel. We can be getting to know their names by now. Also, we can drop in on the new teachers and offer a listening ear. They need our attention.

We are establishing our reputations as teachers. Our top priority is to establish control. Some educators will tell a new teacher the best way to establish control is, "Don't smile until Christmas." Since first impressions are so powerful, I think this is bad advice. We need to show our students that we care about them on day one. We cannot build effective relationships with students unless they know that we care about them. God tells us that we are to love and serve one another. How can we accomplish this without smiling?

This month is also our training and adjustment month. We are training our students to follow rules and procedures. Proper instruction of rules, procedures, and expectations is important to a student's ability to adjust to a new system. A successful adjustment means great potential for academic success.

This is the time of year that we are reminded of the importance of loyalties and team spirit. We are busy supporting our elementary, junior high, high school, college and professional sports teams. We are fiercely loyal toward our teams and our fellow fans. What a great feeling it is to be part of a team!

September also signifies the beginning of autumn with all of the sights, sounds, and smells that go with the season. "Meet the Teacher Night," Open House, PTA activities, and team sports keep us busy in the evenings.

A School is a Haven

A school is a haven for children who:

- are rejected—because they find acceptance with open arms.
- have no hope—because they hear words of encouragement.
- are not loved—because caring relationships are formed.
- are verbally abused—because they hear soft, gentle words.
- are physically abused—because they receive gentle embraces.
- are ridiculed—because they hear words that build confidence.
- have no joy—because they can feel a spirit of happiness.
- are afraid—because they are protected from harm.
- are alone—because friends are found.
- are hurting—because they find a listening ear.
- have given up—because they find partners to help build their hope for a great future.

Our schools truly are havens for some of our children. It is a fact that for some children the only place they receive praise or gain feelings of positive self-worth is at school. There are no other people in their lives that provide them with a loving environment. How fortunate for us educators that we are in a position to enrich the lives of God's children!

Matt Stephen, Ed.D.

Often we find ourselves complaining that there is too little time to teach the academic curriculum because we are also expected to teach values, social rules, and citizenship. Time is our enemy. Where are we supposed to find the time to be mother and father to some of these children? It is fact that our society has moved to a point where an alarming number of parents are abdicating their parental responsibilities. They are only worried about themselves, and they have no inclination to look out for their children's future. So who is left to take over? The public school system is there. As servant leaders, we can look at this as a burden or as an opportunity to serve God's children.

David tells us that God is our refuge:

> The Lord is my rock, my fortress, and my savior;
> my God is my rock, in whom I find protection. He
> is my shield, the strength of my salvation, and my
> stronghold.
>
> Psalm 18:2

We are God's children serving God's children. Just as God is our refuge, we serve as a refuge for his children. We are challenged to respond to his children with the same love and protection that he provides for us.

Dear Father,

Thank you for serving as our refuge. We praise you for knowing our every need and providing comfort for us during our times of distress. Help us to know that through our dedication to you, we can daily provide a refuge for each of your children. Amen.

Let Go and Let God

I have heard the popular saying "Let Go and Let God" many times. It tells me to go to God more often and not be so independent. It tells me that worrying about situations is not nearly as effective as turning them over to God. It is a reminder that we are not in this life by ourselves. This is a great saying, but it is very hard advice to follow.

We are good about striving to include God more in our personal lives; however, we often leave God out of our professional lives. After all, we are required to leave God and religion out of our public schools. In spite of society's demands, God does not leave us on Monday mornings and return to us on Friday evenings. God is on call around the clock seven days a week, even at school. He does not believe in separation of church and state.

We spend a lot of time planning in our jobs. We create daily lesson plans, weekly plans, semester plans, and yearly plans. We plan scopes and sequences for our curriculum so that we accomplish all of our goals each year. We also plan classroom management procedures, student assessments, and extra curricular activities. We plan these activities on our own or in groups. We strive to be successful in our planning efforts for our schools, but it can be frustrating when our planning does not lead to success. We can seek professional help in planning for student success. There is a planning consultant who guarantees his work to produce 100-percent success for all students. He works for free, and he is easy to contact. Perhaps we should rely less upon ourselves and spend more time planning with God.

Matt Stephen, Ed.D.

Here are three major areas of our professional lives in which we can rely more upon God:

1. Student Discipline

We can ask God to help us open our hearts to our children. We can show the love of God by developing caring relationships with our students while we teach them God's values and guiding principles. God will give us the wisdom and patience we need to steer our children's behavior toward his will.

2. Innovative/Creative Instructional Strategies

We can ask God to open our minds to new possibilities and trust that he will inspire us and give us the ideas we need to motivate our children. We can ask for help with our many decisions on how to best instruct our students. God can help us decide just what the children need.

3. Interpersonal Relationships

We can ask God to help us to be patient with one another (students and colleagues) and treat everyone with dignity and respect. All of us need God's guidance and wisdom to be successful servant leaders. Only through strong, interpersonal relationships can we help others grow.

We have been given the ultimate advice about planning:

> Don't worry about anything; instead, pray about everything. Tell God what you need, and thank

him for all he has done. If you do this, you will experience God's peace, which is far more wonderful than the human mind can understand. His peace will guard your hearts and minds as you live in Christ Jesus.

Philippians 4:6–7

We are told to include God in everything we do. Notice that we are not told to try everything we can think of first and then call on God. For true success, we are to call on him for everything. We are also told to check in with a "thank you" when he helps us! Can we afford to pass up on a consultant who works for free and has proven to be 100-percent accurate in all decisions?

Dear Father,

Thank you for your constant presence. Help us to be aware of your presence and consult with you for help in our daily lives. Amen.

Matt Stephen, Ed.D.

The Lighthouse

She is larger-than-life and awe-inspiring
as she stands firmly on the ground.
She slings her light out into the darkness
turning the lost into the found.

Dependable, patient, stalwart, and sturdy
are some words used to express her charm.
She is a beacon of light guiding ships in the night
providing direction and protection from harm.

She guides others on their adventures
some never to return, their futures skillfully erected.
She never abandons her post, she always remains behind
with no accolades expected.

It is often a thankless job …
Yet, she is ever faithful to her mission of serving others.

Please forgive me for getting deep or profound
like some philosopher or preacher,
but it seems to me you could drop the word "lighthouse"
and insert the word "teacher."

Educators can be compared to a lighthouse. We spend our lives guiding children as they pass through our schools. We reach out to our wandering students. We help them learn what they need to know and send them off to bigger and better futures. Hopefully because of us, they will lead richer, more satisfying lives. We give our best effort and receive very little praise, yet our existence is essential. We are the guiding lights that our children depend upon to lead them. We are the lighthouses that guide our children toward their futures. We are the firm foundation of our society that molds the next generation for our country!

Jesus tells us that we are the lights that guide others to him:

> Don't hide your light under a basket! Instead, put it on a stand and let it shine for all. In the same way, let your good deeds shine out for all to see, so that everyone will praise your heavenly Father.
>
> Matthew 5:15–16

Dear Father,

Thank you for making us lighthouses to guide others to you. You are our firm foundation that allows us to weather the storms as we serve your children. Amen.

Reputation Building

Do you remember the reputations of some of your teachers as you were growing up? They were reputed to be easy or hard, nice or mean, and fun or boring. I remember that I knew a lot about some of my teachers before I stepped into their rooms for the first time. It is interesting to note that sometimes the reputations were accurate and sometimes they were not.

Educators have a reputation they must build beginning with the first day they walk into a school building. I remember my first few weeks as a new teacher at a high school. As a young looking twenty-four-year old, it was not uncommon for me to be stopped in the hall by other teachers and asked for my hallway pass (but wait—how many high school kids wear a sport coat and tie?). I knew that I needed to build a tough, no-nonsense reputation with my students (and fellow colleagues) in a hurry or I would lose control. I diligently worked on that reputation for many years. Also, each time I changed jobs or schools, I had to re-establish my reputation with the students and staff. Each time I pursued the establishing of a new reputation, I had a particular one in mind—one to fit the situation.

Everything we do and say on the job is applied toward creating our reputation. Our words and deeds away from our work are also catalogued and added to our reputation. So the pressure is on twenty-four hours a day, seven days a week. What kind of reputation have you built up to this point? What are your children and your colleagues telling others about you? Are you easy or tough, fair or unjust, caring or indifferent, hard working or lazy, fun or boring? Is this reputation the one you set out to earn?

The Bible tells us how to create a good reputation:

> Never let loyalty and kindness get away from you! Wear them like a necklace; write them deep within your heart. Then you will find favor with both God and people, and you will gain a good reputation. Trust in the Lord with all your heart; do not depend on your own understanding. Seek his will in all you do, and he will direct your paths.
>
> Proverbs 3:3–6

We are told that we are not to build our reputations on our own. If we trust only in ourselves, we will fail. We are to put God first in everything that we do. We are to trust in God to help us each step of the way. Only through him can we build the reputation that we need to serve his children according to his will.

Dear Father,

We ask for your guidance as we build our reputations. Help us to earn the reputation of being a fair, hard-working, compassionate, interesting and fun person to have as a teacher. We need a good reputation in order to best serve your children. Amen.

Two Eggs Over-Easy with a
Side Order of Prayer

It is important to start every day with a good, healthy breakfast. Starting the day with a good breakfast improves a person's physical health. A good, healthy breakfast enables our bodies to repair themselves and grow stronger. We need the correct nourishment in order to sustain the energy necessary to function at work and do our best.

As servant leaders, we need more than nourishment for our physical bodies. We need spiritual nourishment as well. Paul tells us how to draw nourishment from our Lord:

> And now, just as you accepted Christ Jesus as your Lord, you must continue to live in obedience to him. Let your roots grow down into him and draw up nourishment from him, so you will grow in faith, strong and vigorous in the truth you were taught. Let your lives overflow with thanksgiving for all he has done.
>
> Colossians 2:6–7

To grow stronger in the Lord, we need to begin each day with prayer. This daily communication with God gives us the needed spiritual energy to supply us with motivation to serve him and his children to the best of our abilities. Talking with God first thing in the morning helps us to maintain our priorities and provides us with the proper focus for the day. Communion with God repairs our spirits and makes us stronger.

Pressured by time, I once headed for school in the mornings with a "donut-type" breakfast in hand. I would also say a "donut-type" prayer asking for God's guidance for the day. A "donut-type" prayer is a quick and insincere prayer (For you donut lovers, please understand this is simply a metaphor—I like donuts). I have learned to eat a hot, nutritious meal to begin the day. It better takes care of my physical body. I have also learned to take the time to commune with God in sincerity each morning to ask for his guidance. This makes all the difference in my spiritual life.

Dear Father,

More important than a good breakfast, we need to start each day with you! Please grant us physical strength and peace of mind. Please help us focus on your will and purpose for this day. Amen.

Matt Stephen, Ed.D.

Be the First

A fourth grade teacher was once told by a parent, "You are the first teacher to say something really nice about my child." I hope this parent was exaggerating; but if not, think about it... a fourth grade teacher hears from a parent that she is the first teacher to say something nice about her child. This would indicate that a child spent four years with professional teachers and staff with little or no positive feedback given to the parents. If no positive comments were made to the parents, one has to wonder if any caring statements were made to the child.

Children form their self-images during the first years of their lives, and they determine their self-worth throughout childhood and adolescence. Their egos are fragile and vulnerable to criticism—or worse, indifference. We have all learned that students perform better if they believe the adults in school care about them. I wager that the teachers you remember the most fondly are those who took the time to demonstrate an interest in you. As servant leaders, our purpose is to see that each child hears what is good about him or her. We are here to save this world one child at a time!

Parents are delighted with us when we demonstrate a true caring attitude toward their children. I have found that I can make mistakes as long as the parents know that I care about their children. If they think I do not care about their children, I can do nothing right. I feel the same way when I am wearing my "parent hat." I will let questionable teaching practices slip by as long as I think the teacher cares about my child.

We are not only here to serve the children and their parents, we are here to delight them. In order to delight a customer, one has to go beyond the customer's expectations for service. Servant leaders know that those who serve others and give generously are rewarded. Paul tells us what happens as a result of our giving to others:

> So, two good things will happen—the needs of the Christians in Jerusalem will be met, and they will joyfully express their thanksgiving to God.
>
> 2 Corinthians 9:12

By serving others, we not only help those who are in need, we inspire others to be thankful to God for dedicated, caring educators. God should receive the thanks for the good that we do for the children. Parents will know to credit God for our good works if we let them know that he is in charge of our lives and our actions.

So what is one way we can go beyond the call of duty to delight our customers? We can enthusiastically praise students for their strengths and good qualities in the presence of their parents. Great things happen as a result of praise: students are motivated to do their best, parents are pleased with the school, and the overall school climate improves.

Servant leaders constantly praise students—the easy as well as the difficult ones. If we show personal interest in them, they will be blessed. We cannot let these opportunities get past us.

Dear Father,

Thank you for the opportunity to teach your children. You are responsible for every good action that we do. We are your hands here on earth. Grant us your wisdom to help us delight your children and their parents. Amen.

Guiding Principles

Each of us has a moral code or a set of values that guides our daily behavior. Sometimes this code is referred to as "guiding principles." From the time we wake up until we go to bed, our guiding principles direct our every thought and action. Our students soon learn through observation which principles guide our behavior. In fact, students often incorporate our guiding principles (good and bad) into their own personalities. Because we are role models for our students, our choice of guiding principles becomes even more crucial.

What guiding principles should educators follow and model for students? Here is a short-list of guiding principles and actions created by some teachers at a brainstorm session:

- Be consistent
- Praise one another
- Encourage and support one another
- Be open-minded
- Be a leader and a follower
- Lead by example
- Listen
- Be reflective and self-evaluative
- Learn from one another
- Keep your sense of humor
- Be dependable
- Be spontaneous
- Work together

Matt Stephen, Ed.D.

- Be friendly
- Be professional
- Keep a positive attitude
- Be dedicated to children
- Keep high expectations
- Be patient
- Go to the source with concerns
- Take advantage of available resources
- Be confidential
- Use tact and diplomatic language
- Be trusting
- Be willing to account for your actions
- Forgive and forget
- Be humble
- Don't forget to apologize
- Keep people informed
- Teach mastery, not material
- Be willing to go "the extra mile"
- Don't forget to take care of your personal life
- Be willing to give and accept criticism with a spirit of love
- Be empathetic
- Be willing to ask questions
- Respect one another's differences and opinions and strive for unity
- Be fair

It is easy to see how these guiding principles can bring success to educators, but this is quite a checklist for everyday behavior! Can we possibly follow all of these guiding principles every minute of every day? Without God's help, it doesn't seem likely.

Jesus tells us how effective we are without him:

> Remain in me, and I will remain in you. For a branch cannot produce fruit if it is severed from the vine, and you cannot be fruitful apart from me.
>
> John 15:4

We are promised that alone we will not be fruitful; thus, we will not be able to serve God's children to his expectations. As we live in the Lord, we are empowered to do more than we think is humanly possible. Through Jesus, we can successfully follow these guiding principles each day and provide the best possible role model for his children. We can call upon the Lord each morning to ask for his guidance, peace, wisdom, and strength.

Dear Father,

Through you, all things are possible. We need your guidance to maintain the highest of personal standards for ourselves. Only with your help can we be superhuman and near-perfect models for your children. Amen.

Looking Past the Bad to See the Sad

All of us have shared the frustration of teaching children who exhibit chronic misbehavior. Sometimes our efforts to change a student's behavior fail and the problems seem to get worse each day. These behavior challenges can sometimes consume our lives and make us wish we had pursued another profession. I have seen many good teachers leave the profession, not because of the long hours or the short pay, but because of difficult children. How do we deal with a child who is so adept at disrupting other people's lives?

Paul gives us an answer:

> All praise to the God and Father of our Lord Jesus Christ. He is the source of every mercy and the God who comforts us. He comforts us in all our troubles so that we can comfort others. When others are troubled, we will be able to give them the same comfort God has given us.
>
> 2 Corinthians 1:3–4

As servant leaders, we are told to comfort those who are in trouble. In order to be a comforter, we must look past the "bad" in a child and see the "sad" in a child. Behind every incorrigible behavior problem is a hurt child. We must find the hurt. Once we find the deep-rooted, inner reason for a child's misbehavior, we can begin to change that behavior. We know this process takes valuable time that we sometimes feel we do not have.

It is easy to punish children for their misbehavior. The easiest punishment is to separate the child from the rest of the population through time out, detention, suspension, assignment to alternative schools and expulsion. These actions work for the short-term, but they do not provide long-term solutions. It takes time and effort to diagnose the true reasons behind the misbehavior and devise a plan to teach the student behavior that will help him or her succeed. We must take the time to build important relationships and teach the children self-discipline. We, the adults, must initiate this process because students do not know how to take the first steps toward more successful behavior.

The very wise King Solomon once said:

> Teach your children to choose the right path, and
> when they are older, they will remain upon it.
> Proverbs 22:6

God plainly tells us that we are to comfort those who are in trouble, not to send them away. He also tells us to raise children in his way and not to give up on them. As servant leaders, we know this will cost us our time, but we are willing to give it. Our love and attention can be the catalyst for true, positive change in our children's lives.

Dear Father,

Help us to love others as you love us. Please give us the wisdom to know how to properly guide your children and the patience to effectively build these vital, personal relationships. Amen.

Test of Fortitude

One morning at school I was verbally assaulted by a very angry mother in the middle of the main hallway. Her perception was that her children were being mistreated by some of the school staff; and as she continued to speak, she became very abusive with her language. She refused my requests to carry the conversation to my office, and she continued to yell and curse. Finally, in a very trashy manner, she yelled out some very foul words assaulting my character (including the "f-word") and stormed out of the building.

My emotional side said to have her barred from the campus and to file verbal assault charges with the police. My professional side said to deal firmly with the situation, but to also do my best to mend the school-parent relationship so the children would not suffer. My professional side won out. Through several phone calls and meetings, I was able to help the mother understand a better way to express her concerns.

On my way home that night, I asked myself (and not for the first time), "Why do I pour my heart and soul into this job only to be treated like this?" After brooding over this question for several hours, the answer hit me. I remembered that toward the end of the day a fourth grade student came up to me in the hallway and asked me if I was okay. I asked him what he meant by that. He said, "You know.... about this morning." Obviously, he had witnessed the event that morning, and he was concerned about me! Now I remember why I put up with the pain.... because of students like this.

God promises us that trials and tribulations can strengthen us:

> We can rejoice, too, when we run into problems and trials, for we know that they are good for us— they help us to learn to endure.
>
> Romans 5:3

It is important to note that we are told that we should not merely endure tribulations; we should glory in them! We should cheerfully face challenges and be thankful for them. God gives us his strength and allows us to transcend the problems of the world when we focus on his will. It is our faith in God that helps us win the daily battles. Each struggle makes us stronger and better able to carry out our mission to serve God and his children.

God also tells us that when we go through fiery trials; just like precious metals, we emerge purer than before:

> But he knows where I am going. And when he has tested me like gold in a fire, he will pronounce me innocent.
>
> Job 23:10

It is exciting to know that our daily struggles can purify us and better prepare us to serve others. I like to think that all experiences in our lives have a purpose. Our reactions to these experiences make all the difference. Adverse experiences can either build us up or tear us down. The decision is ours.

Matt Stephen, Ed.D.

Dear Father,

Help us to concentrate on the joy of serving others and not the pain that sometimes comes with it. Help us to see the good in everyone and everything. Thank you for each adventure that we experience. Give us the wisdom and strength to use these experiences to make us stronger and better able to serve you. Amen.

Hugology

As an educator, I have researched "Hugology" (the study of hugs) for years. Spending countless hours in the field observing and experiencing various kinds of hugs, I found there is much to be learned from them. I have become an expert, and I would like to share the theory of Hugology with you.

Hugs can be classified according to their meaning. In the realm of adult hugging, there are several types of hugs. First there is the "Hello, how are you? I haven't seen you in a long time" hug. This hug usually takes two to three seconds and can be of rough and sometimes rib-bruising caliber. Second, there is the "I really care about you, but I don't want to start any rumors" hug. This hug also averages two to three seconds in length, but it is gentler and more intimate. Then there is the "I love you and don't care what others think" hug. This hug ranges in length according to the situation (five seconds and longer). This type of hug is reserved for special people in our lives.

Children's hugs can also be categorized according to their meaning. First there is the "Hi, great to see you, but I've got to hurry" hug. This hug can range from .001 to 2.0 seconds depending on the urgency. These hugs can often leave bruises or telltale marks (during the flu/cold season when noses are running, these hugs can lead to expensive cleaning bills). The second kind of hug is the "I'm really glad to know you" hug. These hugs last approximately two to five seconds. I like these hugs because they are sincere. Then, occasionally one gets the "I need you, please protect me" hug. This is a very important hug not to ignore. This

Matt Stephen, Ed.D.

hug can last up to several minutes. We have all been there and know these hugs.

I believe that God put us on this world to supply these protective hugs when they are needed. They pop up at the strangest times for usual and unusual reasons. Children are much more likely to ask for them than adults are, but adults need them just the same. It is easy to recognize a child's need for a protective hug because he/she won't let go! Adults won't ask for hugs as freely as children, so with older students and adults, one needs to be more attune to signals. There is one irrefutable fact about protective hugs—verbal communication is not necessary. Taking the time to gently hold someone says it all. One day I gave a routine hug, but the child would not let go. We hugged for a few seconds longer without any words said. Nevertheless, something was loudly communicated by that hug, "You are important and I care about you."

In today's world, physical touching can quickly become tragic. If someone mistakes the meaning of physical contact, untold problems can occur. This is a scary concept for educators because we work each day with children who outwardly demand or secretly desire hugs. When I was a first-year teacher (twenty-four years old), I found one of my students, a sixteen-year-old girl, crying in the hallway. She asked for a hug. Acutely aware of the social and professional ramifications, I told her that I cared about her but that she would have to settle for a "mental hug." At the time, I saw this as the safe thing to do, but now I look back on it and wonder if I missed an opportunity to share God's love.

Paul tells us that we should express love for one another:

> I pray that your love for each other will overflow more and more, and that you will keep on growing in your knowledge and understanding.
>
> Philippians 1:9

How can we overflow with love for one another and not show it through gentle touches or hugs? Let's never give up on showing love for one another. If we utilize God's wisdom, we should be able to use loving touch and gentle words to show his love for our children. It is my hope and prayer that if we touch others out of genuine love and concern, God will protect us from false accusations.

Dear Father,

Thank you for putting us in a situation where we can share your love daily with your children. Help us to be aware of others' needs and to always be ready to express your love with opened arms. Please protect us from harm as we show your love to others. Amen.

October

October is a month for getting into a routine. We have established our rules and procedures, and the students have had time to acclimate themselves to the teachers and to one another.

It is time to get to know the parents. The first grading period often ends during October. By now, we know the students well enough to conference with parents about their needs. We can contact the parents of each student and give them our assessment of where their child is academically. Phone calls, newsletters, personal notes, and parent conferences are easy ways to show parents that we are dedicated to their child's success. Here is our opportunity to be the first to compliment children in front of their parents. It is imperative to get a positive contact in before something negative occurs. We can show God's love and our dedication to his children by involving their parents. How we communicate with our children and their parents clearly demonstrates whether or not God is working through our lives.

Fun activities such as Homecoming, Fall Festivals, and Halloween keep us busy. We also concentrate on activities such as Fire Prevention Week, Red Ribbon Week, National School Lunch Week, and School Bus Safety Week. These activities help us to focus on our often-overlooked food service and transportation employees. Usually in October there are so many activities going on that we get frustrated and wonder, "When are we supposed to teach?" Keep in mind that some of these activities remain in the children's minds for the rest of their lives. Unfortunately, they do not remember our day-to-day learning routines.

The changing leaves and onset of colder weather give this month a special flavor. We begin to curl up with good books on weekends instead of looking for outdoor activities. This is a good time to reflect again on our guiding principles and how they affect our daily thoughts and actions. We are the shining lights that lead the way for God's children. We can continue to ask God for his guidance, strength, wisdom and peace.

A Lesson from Mother Nature

The other day at a red light, I witnessed a bird swooping down on cars as they entered the intersection. I wondered what this "crazy" bird was doing until I noticed an exact replica lying very still in the middle of the intersection. I realized this bird was trying to protect its mate who was seriously injured or dead. Imagine the determination of this several-ounce bird as it charged these moving vehicles weighing several thousand pounds each! I know this bird did not fully understand the situation, but it had no problem challenging objects much bigger than itself. This bird illustrated to me the definition of true determination, courageously going up against great odds to achieve a purpose!

Educators sometimes battle against great odds. We are often confronted with children who are not motivated to learn or behave at school. Many of our children have severe learning, physical, or emotional disabilities. Educators often receive confusing information regarding new programs, curriculum development or instructional strategies. Some teachers are challenged with a shortage of equipment and supplies or inadequate facilities. To add to our frustrations, we are often criticized by society for not working miracles fast enough. As hopeless as some of these situations may seem, we continue to do what we know is right. I admire educators for their determination, drive, and service spirit. I see it in them every day!

Paul tells us about winning attitudes:

Remember that in a race everyone runs, but only one person gets the prize. You also must run in such a way that you will win. All athletes practice strict self-control. They do it to win a prize that will fade away, but we do it for an eternal prize.

1 Corinthians 9:24–25

Paul says that if we are in the race, we should be in it to win. There is no doubt that we are in a race for our children's future. We compete against the many exciting activities that society has to offer. We are often tempted to give up because of the great odds against us; but by dropping out of the race, we will never experience the thrill of victory as we win our children for God. Miracles cannot happen through us if we do not try. Alone, we do not have the power to perform miracles; but with God's help, nothing is impossible. Faith in God, even a small amount such as the size of a mustard seed, is the key to moving mountains.

Jesus tells us to have faith:

> Then Jesus told them, "I assure you if you have faith, and don't doubt, you can do things like this and much more. You can even say to this mountain, 'May God lift you up and throw you into the sea,' and it will happen."

Matthew 21:21

With faith in God, we can move mountains and charge moving vehicles!

Dear Father,

Thank you for putting us in such an important profession. Keep us filled with the service spirit so that we never give up. Running the race to win your children is enough reason to give 100 percent all of the time. Help us to continue to move those mountains and charge those moving vehicles. Amen.

Time for Trifocals

Educators are problem solvers. As we work in our classrooms or work places, we must look at all problems that arise through a set of trifocals. We can consider our own point of view as well as the points of view of our students and their parents when we study these problems and search for solutions. If we are able to do this, we will save ourselves a countless number of headaches.

Any time I look at a problem from another point of view, I am able to gain a different understanding. Once I was trying to deal with a child who had severe emotional problems. He would curse and strike out at other children as well as adults. In a meeting with the parents, despite numerous testimonies regarding this child's behavior, the parents stood firm that their child would never curse or become violent. The parents refused to admit to the possibility of a problem; therefore, they were not amenable to seeking a solution. I was at a loss! I left the meeting frustrated and with little hope of getting the child any help. After I donned my trifocals, I came to the realization that this was the parents' way of demonstrating unconditional love and loyalty toward their child. This was their way of protecting him. Although the problem was never resolved, I at least came to understand why the parents seemed to be so uncooperative. This realization helped me in future encounters where people seemed to be quite unreasonable.

When approaching a problem, it is important that we look through our trifocals to examine the situation from all sides. One can look through trifocals by following these steps:

Matt Stephen, Ed.D.

1. Listen to all perceptions (student, parent, and staff).

2. Accept these perceptions as reality for those people who own them.

3. Let the other parties know that you understand their feelings and that you care about them.

4. Work together on a solution.

These steps are helpful when we are trying to understand children, teenagers, or adults. One doesn't have to agree with another person's perception in order to work out a solution to a problem. We can agree to disagree about the reason for a problem while we agree to collaborate on a solution.

Peter tells us how to treat one another:

> Finally, all of you should be of one mind, full of sympathy toward each other, loving one another with tender hearts and humble minds.
>
> 1 Peter 3:8

Living together as one big happy family is a tall order these days. A family of several billion members on this planet will be hard to keep happy, but we can give it a try. No doubt, tenderness and humility will go a long way to helping us accomplish peace within the family.

Dear Father,

Fill us with sympathy, love, and understanding toward one another. We will strive to keep a tender heart and a humble mind as we approach our problems and seek solutions. Amen.

Dignity

We have all heard the expression, "Don't sink to the other person's level." These are good words to help us fashion our servant leadership style. Jesus supported this saying when he told us to turn the other cheek when we are accosted by others. Unfortunately, there are some people out there who need to release their frustrations over something in their personal lives, and they decide that teachers are perfect victims because they have to take it. They are relatively sure that teachers won't retaliate in the same hateful manner that they are exhibiting. They are right; we are above that type of behavior! I do not believe that the "other cheek" theory means that we should be human punching bags. I have always believed that one of the main purposes of the campus administrator is to protect teachers from meanspirited people.

The three guiding principles that I live by are dignity, service, and excellence. Dignity is the most important principle because without it, the other two cannot exist. Studies show that once stripped of their dignity, people cannot learn. The part of the brain responsible for learning shuts down when one loses dignity because the brain goes into a defensive mode. The brain focuses on attempts to recapture personal dignity. Under these conditions, constructive communications come to a halt and relationships can be damaged. Without personal dignity for students, the principles of providing service and striving for excellence in schools cannot exist.

Maintaining students' dignity means we should treat them as we want to be treated. Granting dignity is accomplished through using gentle words, giving freedom with responsibility, demonstrating caring attitudes, enjoying fun and laughter, granting importance, and developing friendships. We adults want these things. If they are important for adults, they are important for children. Dignity is not speaking or acting out of anger. It is not over-controlling children. It is not being unfeeling or uncaring. I have learned over the years that parents will forgive us for not being perfect educators if we treat their children with dignity and respect. If parents decide that we do not care about their children, no amount of talk can save the relationship.

Allowing fellow adults to maintain their dignity is also important. Often, it means keeping one's mouth closed. Words hastily spoken in anger always hurt us. Speaking against each other erodes team spirit and damages relationships. The best approach is a private, face-to-face conversation with the intent of solving the problem. If a problem is approached in a calm, positive, constructive manner, everyone can win. Only if we retain our own dignity and allow others to maintain their dignity, can we truly work together and support one another. Sinking to a meanspirited person's level might feel good temporarily, but it will only escalate the problem.

Paul tells us to be in the business of supporting people:

> So encourage each other and build each other up,
> just as you are already doing.
>
> 1 Thessalonians 5:11

We should please others. If we do what helps them, we will build them up in the Lord.

Romans 15:2

We are told to spend our time and effort serving and building up other people. We are in the perfect position to dignify many people: students, parents, coworkers, and community members. By upholding the dignity of others and ourselves, we can ensure a successful learning environment for our children. We can depend upon God, with a little help from servant leader administrators, to protect us from the meanspirited people looking for punching bags!

Dear Father,

Help us to always maintain our own dignity while we preserve the dignity of others. Thank you for supportive colleagues. Together we will build a caring, supportive, and successful learning environment for your children. Amen.

Right at the End of Your Nose

Many answers in life are obvious. They are right at the end of our noses. So why don't we always see them? Sometimes we cannot see the simplest of solutions to our challenges because we are too close to the situation. We often have a personal stake or personal involvement that prevents us from seeing the situation clearly. Our tunnel vision often restricts our view of the problem; therefore, the range of solutions is also restricted. Quite often, we need to step back from our situations and examine the obvious.

So how do we do this? We can slow down and allow time for ourselves to examine the problem and possible solutions. Sometimes patience over a period of time allows problems to work themselves out. Another possibility is to ask someone else for advice or insight into the problem. Sometimes another perspective is all that is needed to see the obvious solution. I cannot tell you how many times I have asked someone for some insight on a solution only to receive a strange look because the solution was so obvious to everyone but me!

Teams are great problem solvers. I have witnessed on countless occasions when a team of people was able to find a solution that none of the individual members could have found alone. Although we sometimes cannot see a solution at the end of our own nose, we can identify a solution at the end of someone else's nose. Moreover, if someone spots a solution at the end of our nose that we cannot see, it is best not to let our nose get out-of-joint. We are all here to watch one another's noses.

The never-fail solution is to ask God for his intervention. James told us almost two thousand years ago:

> If you need wisdom—if you want to know what God wants you to do—ask him, and he will gladly tell you. He will not resent your asking.
>
> James 1:5

Our answers are right at the end of our noses. God tells us simply to be aware that he is God, he knows what is best, and he will give us the answers. All we need to do is go to him for solutions to our problems.

Dear Father,

You have the answers to all of our problems. Please give us the wisdom to know that we cannot solve all problems by ourselves and the patience to slow down and seek your guidance. Amen.

Teacher-Parent Conferences

Teacher-parent conferences can tie people's stomachs in knots. In some cases, both teachers and parents can come to dread these meetings. Although everyone shares the common goal to help children, these meetings can often become contentious and unpleasant. I have spent many restless moments, both as a teacher and as an administrator, worrying about upcoming teacher-parent conferences.

Imagine a child in the center of an old rickety step-bridge that stretches across a deep ravine. The bridge is about to collapse and the child needs help. The child's parents enter the bridge from one end. The educators from the child's school enter the bridge from the other end. Everyone meets in the middle. The parents and educators discuss how to help the child off the bridge, but they cannot come to an agreement. As they talk, they slowly back away from the child. Eventually, the parents and the educators are yelling at one another from opposite sides of the ravine. As they point fingers at one another, the bridge collapses and the child falls. All that is left to do is to look at one another and issue blame for the loss of the child. It is obvious that no one wins in this scenario, but it happens more often than we would like to admit.

We often get into battles just like this one. As professionals, we know the educational research; and we have observed the children in the school setting. We want the parents to sit back and listen to our professional knowledge. The parents have great personal knowledge about their children. They know their children better than anyone does, and they want to be heard. Many of the disagreements that parents and educators have are not over educational issues; rather they are about who has the most power. The real issues about the children sometimes get lost in battles for power.

Parenting and teaching are equally difficult jobs. Educators with personal children know this to be true. All stakeholders need to be allowed to play part in school decisions about children. Shared decision-making is difficult to achieve because both parents and educators hesitate to relinquish the power of their positions. Sometimes the parents are at a loss for what to do. They want to let the professionals do what they do best, but they also want their feelings and efforts to be recognized as valuable to the child's well-being. These feelings can result in defensive, blaming, or controlling actions.

Jesus told us that those who are humble will receive the greatest of rewards:

> God blesses those who realize their need for him,
> for the Kingdom of Heaven is given to them.
> Matthew 5:3

As servant leaders, we can ensure that each child wins. Through a spirit of humility and cooperation, we can form an alliance between parents and schools that will lead to successful partnerships. Through these partnerships, we can truly serve our students and help them build their best future!

Dear Father,

We know that we are not the experts in everything. Help us to keep an open mind and allow others a role in making decisions about students. Your children are the ones who will benefit from our partnerships. Amen.

Hello World

Isn't it funny that we educators already know what our greatest problem is, yet we do nothing about it? Our greatest fault is also our greatest asset—we do not let go! We eat, sleep, think, and breathe education. We talk about education until our spouses and friends beg us to change the subject. We focus on our work to the point that we become consumed, and we subject ourselves to early burnout.

Not only are we consumed with education, we often focus on the negative aspects of the profession. We try to stay positive, but let's face it; our conversations about education can often turn sour. It is no wonder we burn out! If we are constantly subjected to negativity, we can lose our service spirit. I once heard of a principal who adamantly refused to talk education while on break, at lunch, or outside the school. What a gutsy move he made in an attempt to have a life outside of education!

It is important that we change our focus when we are away from work. There is a great big beautiful world out there that doesn't revolve around education. We should say, "Hello" to it and introduce ourselves. We can plan extra-curricular activities for ourselves during the week such as participating in church and community organizations, volunteering for charities, fellowshipping with friends, competing through sports, and occupying our time with hobbies. These life-enhancing activities may serve to save us from education burnout. We can also keep a watchful eye on our colleagues to see if they are burning out. We can protect one another by involving ourselves in these extra curricular activities together.

Matt Stephen, Ed.D.

Jesus tells us how to beat burnout:

> Then Jesus said, "Come to me, all of you who are weary and carry heavy burdens, and I will give you rest.
>
> Matthew 11:28

Our Lord knows that life is tough. He promises to give us respite from the weariness of the world if we will hand our lives over to him. He knows how hard we work, and he wants to shelter us from burnout. All we have to do is go to him.

Dear Father,

We know that you will give us rest. We sometimes become very weary from the challenging task of serving your children. Remind us to seek a life outside of education and come to you for rest. Amen.

Situational Leadership

As teachers, we know that one leadership style is not going to fit all situations in the classroom. Different situations determine what we must do and how we must act. We are called upon to be directors, experts, explorers, facilitators, mentors, consultants, or even spectators in the classroom. One can certainly say that leading students is not boring. It is a job filled with variety and on-the-job training.

God recognizes that there are many different and appropriate ways for us to act:

> There is a time for everything, a season for every activity under heaven.
>
> Ecclesiastes 3: 1

God tells us there is a time to be born and die, plant and harvest, kill and heal, cry and laugh, grieve and dance, tear and mend, war and peace, love and hate, etc. God wants us to understand that we cannot approach everything in the same manner. As servant leaders, we can ask ourselves, "How will I lead today? Will I be forceful or gentle, demanding or understanding, dictator or team player, driven or relaxed, diplomatic or blunt, sympathetic or hard-nosed, fun-loving or serious?" The truth is we will be all of these at one time or another. What must not change is our attitude toward others. Regardless of our actions for the moment, we must always keep our Christian attitude toward other people in place.

The one constant that our children should be able to count on is our desire to treat them right. They should know that they will always be important to us and their dignity will always be preserved. With this attitude as a foundation, our leadership style can never fail us. Using "godliness" as our foundation, our leadership will always be effective.

Dear Father,

Thank you for today. I am not sure of the actions I will take today as a leader; however, I promise to maintain a Christian attitude and share your love with your children. Amen.

Right Action, Wrong Reason

One day at a movie theater a large, scruffy-looking man sat right in front of my wife just as the lights began to dim for the previews. As it was impossible to see over or around his large hair and cowboy hat, my wife politely asked him if he would mind removing his hat. Without even looking at her, he grumbled, "No, I ain't gonna move my hat." My wife leaned back and looked at me as I mentally considered my options. I could:

1. Pull his hat off of his head for him

2. Say something equally rude

3. Speak to him regarding his rudeness and uncaring attitude

4. Quietly get up and move

With the greatest restraint, I chose to move and we shifted over several seats. This was easy to do, as the theater was only half-full.

Later, as I reflected over this incident, I was annoyed with myself that I did not confront the man over his selfish attitude. I thought he needed to be told how rude he was, but I needed to avoid a scene. Moreover, I could smell alcohol on his breath, and it was quite obvious to me that any action on my part would have ended in severe trouble. I could envision the newspaper headlines the next morning: "Local Principal Arrested for Brawling in Family Movie Theater." This was not the kind of behavior our community looks for in the leaders of their children, so I moved to another seat. I told myself that I did the right thing.

Now I realize that I did the right thing, but for the wrong reason. I avoided a confrontation due to fear of tarnishing my reputation. I should have avoided a confrontation out of kindness toward that poor man. I should have felt compassion for him because of his sadness and anger toward the world. In his own way, he was crying out for help, and I was too concerned with my own reputation to help him.

We are constantly telling our students to do the right thing because it's the right thing to do, not from fear of punishment for doing wrong. We want them to follow our society's laws out of understanding and respect rather than avoiding punishment. However, we don't always follow that advice. How many of us stay within the speed limit or buckle up mostly to avoid a traffic ticket? Do we sometimes roll through stop signs? Do we sometimes fudge with insurance companies or the IRS?

We are told throughout the Bible to do what is right, and Paul carries that message a little further:

> Keep a close watch on yourself and on your teaching. Stay true to what is right, and God will save you and those who hear you.
>
> 1 Timothy 4:16

We are promised that God will bless us and use us to help others if we remain true to doing what is right. We are blessed by God if our intentions are true to his will, and God knows our intentions. As servant leaders, we cannot afford to lose this blessing. We are charged to lead others and provide a Christian role model for dealing with conflict. If we follow God's will with correct actions and intentions, we stand to win eternal life for ourselves and those who follow us. There is no greater leadership than this.

Dear Father,

Please give us the patience, strength, and self-control that we need to avoid unnecessary confrontations. Also, help us to match the right attitudes with the right actions. Amen.

Matt Stephen, Ed.D.

Pass It On

Have you ever wondered what our purpose is here on earth? It is hard to focus on one purpose in life when there are so many different directions one's life can take. We are faced with many decisions and options. Our freedom to choose our own fate can overwhelm us and lead us to ponder our ultimate destiny. Even with freedom of choice and multiple directions in which to journey, one single most important purpose in life does exist. We are here to play a simple child's game called "Pass It On." Only we do not play the game by sitting in a circle and passing on whispered words, we play the game by passing on God's love. We know that others need to experience God's love, and we are tasked to introduce God's love to them.

Our task as educators is to teach children. Our mission as a child of God is to share his love. Jesus told us of the greatest commandment:

> Jesus replied, "You must love the Lord your God will all your heart, all your soul, and all your mind. This is the first and greatest commandment. A second is equally important: Love your neighbor as yourself."
>
> Matthew 22: 37–39

As servant leaders, we are in the perfect position to teach children to love God, to love others, and to love themselves. "Teach children to love God?" you ask. "Not in public school, thank you very much! Do not forget about separation of church and state." Our wise forefathers knew that religious freedom would be impossible if the government controlled our religious practices. In our usual confused manner, we have made it almost criminal to talk about God to our children in public schools. However, it is not a crime to show God's love to his children. In fact, we are specifically charged to do just that:

> Dear children, let us stop just saying we love each other; let us really show it by our actions.
>
> 1 John 3:18

It is not a crime to share God's love by teaching the children values such as courage, conviction, respect, courtesy, honesty, patience, truth, responsibility, thoughtfulness, and self-discipline. Everything we do and say each day should reflect our love for God and our desire to share his love with others:

> And whatever you do or say, let it be as a representative of the Lord Jesus, all the while giving thanks through him to God the Father.
>
> Colossians 3:17

Even though talking about God is not always accepted in our schools, we must do what is right. We are charged to spread God's love to everyone around us. We are privileged to play the ultimate "Pass It On" game here on earth, and our profession gives us a great playing field!

Dear Father,

Thank you for your perfect love. Help us to pass that love on to others every minute of each day. Amen.

Matt Stephen, Ed.D.

Coffee, Tea, or Technology?

One morning I was enjoying an excellent breakfast and good conversation with a waitress at a local restaurant. We were talking about the evolution of service in America. She pointed to the coffee urn at the table as an example of how service has changed. She stated that the coffee urn provides the customer with the convenience of immediate coffee refills, but it reduces the interaction between waitresses and customers. She said that she misses the conversations that often resulted from refilling her customers' coffee cups. In our efforts to automate service, we are drastically reducing our interactions with one another. This is one example of how our society is slowly "progressing" itself out of human relationships.

Another reason for a reduction in human interaction and relationship building is our advancement in technology. We can all agree that technology is a great thing, and that it is improving our lives in many ways. It allows for faster service, business transactions, and communications; however, technology is also responsible for a serious decline in the quality of human relations. Have any of your personal relationships been hampered by television, PDAs, fax machines, video games, computers, emails, the Internet and/or cell phones? I still laugh to myself about the day I saw two people eating together in a restaurant. Each one spent the entire time on their cell phones texting others rather than engaging each other in eye-to-eye conversation. I also laugh about the co-workers in adjacent cubicles who email each other rather than talk.

The rapid speed of interaction created by technology does not give us time to get to know one another well. Without prolonged personal interactions, strong relationships cannot be built or maintained. Technology also reduces our need to meet one another face-to-face. We no longer need to personally interact with bank tellers, gas station attendants, phone receptionists, pharmacists, etc. It is easier to be indifferent toward people with whom we are not in close contact. I find it easier to hang up the phone on someone than to shut the door in his or her face. When we find ourselves face-to-face with others, we tend to be more compassionate and empathetic. This loss of quality personal interaction is devastating to our relationship-building processes.

Can technology and high quality human relationships co-exist? Of course, but it will take an extra effort on our part to see that technology does not replace our desire to personally know and serve one another. James tells us why we should commit to one another right away:

> How do you know what will happen tomorrow? For you life is like the morning fog—it's here a little while, then it's gone.
>
> James 4:14

As James so aptly puts it, our lives here on earth are extremely short. We have precious little time to establish our relationships, serve others, and prepare for our eternal life with God. Technology can either help or hinder our efforts to serve on another. We make the decision. We can choose to talk to people who are sitting at the restaurant table with us. We can choose not to answer a cell phone in the middle of a personal conversation. We can choose to pick up the phone or make a personal visit rather than send an email.

Dear Father,

Thank you for our wonderful advances in technology. Help us to manage these advances so that our relationships with one another are not damaged. Although our time here is short, we can still strive to improve our relationships. Help us to value each minute with others as we share your love. Amen.

November

November is a month for continued relationship building with students, parents, and colleagues. A special emphasis on family, friendship, and thankfulness is presented to us through the holidays of Veteran's Day and Thanksgiving Day. This month gives us a great opportunity to model God's grace and teach children to be thankful for God's blessings and other people's sacrifices. Election Day, Youth Appreciation Week, American Education Week, National Geography Awareness Week, and National Children's Book Week all offer good excuses to do something different and exciting for students.

The newness of the school year has definitely worn off at this point. We are well into our established patterns. The first twinges of burnout can begin to hit. It has been ten weeks since the beginning of school, and we have six weeks to go before Winter Break. We are tired, yet there is so much work to do in our professional and personal lives. In effort to stave off burnout, we can be sure to wear our trifocals and look at all situations through other points of view. Also, we can remember to play "Pass It On" and keep charging those moving vehicles. I am sure that God is pleased with our hard work and sacrifice as we help raise his children.

The December holiday celebrations are beginning to loom ever more closely. The stores are well stocked by now, and the spirit of the season is upon us. After the Thanksgiving holidays, it is even more of a challenge to keep the students focused on their studies. This month is an important part of their academic climb because we are preparing to close out the first half of the school year and students need a final push to succeed.

Keep in constant touch with God. Let him know what you need in order to best serve his children.

Surely You Jest

Humor is a terrific motivator, yet we do not engage in it nearly enough. Do you laugh with your students? Do you pull pranks, act silly, dress up in costumes, dance, sing songs, or tell jokes? Do you do the unexpected? Do you lie on the floor, sit on desks, and sometimes break the rules? Do your students think sometimes that you have taken leave of your senses? If you do any of these things, you do them because you enjoy kids. You know that you sometimes have to be a little wild and crazy to get the students' attention and get them interested in what you want them to do.

In order to do these things, we have to like ourselves as well as our students. We have to be spontaneous and choose to have fun. We also have to be self-assured and willing to expose our vulnerable selves. We have to be humble and able to laugh at ourselves. In other words, we must have a sense of humor. During my illustrious career as an administrator, I sang and danced for the students, appeared in faculty plays, dressed up and impersonated famous characters, and told jokes … all rather badly I must admit. As silly as these things were, the students will remember these events forever.

Our children thrive on humor. Look at how much they laugh with one another! We think that most of their humor is off base, but they get to freely choose their own brand of humor (our parents thought our humor was weird, also). Our students constantly incorporate humor into everything they do. I am sorry to say that we tend to lose our sense of humor as we grow older and get more serious about life.

We are told what a sense of humor will do for us:

A cheerful heart is good medicine, but a broken spirit saps a person's strength.

Proverbs 17:22

A cheerful heart will keep us healthy and happy, but without it, we tend to "dry up." If one is bored or unhappy with life and nothing seems to be working, a good way to get healthier is to pick up some medicine in the form of books on humor and look at life through the eyes of humorists. They have a great way of minimizing problems through the use of laughter. If we are taking life too seriously, we can stop and find the humor inside of us. Let's shake our students up by hitting them with some unexpected humor. They will be delighted, and they will remember us always!

Dear Father,

Thank you for humor. It is what keeps us healthy, happy and alive. Help us not to outgrow humor. We will strive to keep a cheerful heart as we serve your children. Amen.

Respect

I have heard teachers say, "I don't care whether or not the students like me as long as they respect me," and I have heard administrators say, "I don't care whether or not the teachers like me as long as they respect me." On the surface, these leaders are saying that they believe that if they must choose between respect and admiration, they believe that respect is more necessary to their success than admiration. Is it possible that these leaders are making these statements in order to give themselves permission to avoid building positive relationships with the people around them?

As experienced servant leaders, we know that respect from others does not just come with the leadership package. It must be earned. It cannot be demanded or bought. For servant leaders, "like" and "respect" go hand-in-hand. Servant leaders do not have to choose between the two because they earn both from their followers. As servant leaders, we treat people as we would like to be treated ourselves, thus we earn the respect from our followers as well as their admiration and devotion. Mutual respect and admiration are the rewards we receive for building positive, personal relationships with our followers.

God is in charge of all leaders here on earth:

> You slave owners must be just and fair to your slaves.
> Remember that you also have a Master—in heaven.
> Colossians 4:1

In God's eyes, all of his children are equal. A position of leadership does not make us better than those who follow. If we are not fair and just with our employees and students, we will one day answer to our Master in heaven.

We can be fair and just with our students by giving them opportunities for power, significance, and a sense of accomplishment. These actions empower students to build self-respect. Once they feel respect for themselves, they can in turn appreciate and respect the people who granted them that power. Thus, mutual respect is born! I once had a student tell me, "Mr. Stephen, I don't know why, but I respect you." I told him it is probably because we can see eye-to-eye and understand each other (in other words, we had built a positive relationship between the two of us).

Dear Father,

Thank you for granting me dignity and treating me with fairness and kindness. Help me to be fair and kind toward others just as you are toward me. Amen.

Crying Over Spilt Children

My preacher asked an interesting question one Sunday, "When did you last cry over the loss of someone?" He was not referring to a person's death, but to their being lost emotionally or spiritually. I could not help but think of the difficult children that I have encountered throughout my career. Many of them were lost because of their upbringing. Through no fault of their own, they developed destructive attitudes toward themselves, others, and life in general. As a result, they were not very lovable or even likable.

I wish I had cried over these students. Instead, I got angry with them for the things that they did. The easiest way to deal with them was removal from the classroom. This allowed them to be isolated and punished while the rest of the students continued with their studies. Once removed, these "trouble makers" could be forgotten for a while. If we were lucky, these disruptive students would move away or drop out before they came back to class.

I am sure that Jesus often cried over what he saw. Many of the people he came across must have caused him great sadness because they had strayed so far from God's will. Yet, he stayed with them and told them how important they were to his Father. He also showed them how much they meant to him by comforting their sorrows and being with them. Our Lord and Savior, the King of Kings, spent time with the lowest of mortal man. He was criticized often for this, but he knew the importance of showing everyone that they were worthy of his love and attention.

Jesus demonstrated this perfect love to me, yet I refused to spend a small amount of time trying to help some of his troubled children. It was easy to overlook these children and focus on those students who showed more promise. Perhaps I could have made a difference in their lives if I had taken the time to cry over them.

Jesus tells us why it is important not to ignore those in need:

> And he will answer, "I assure you, when you refused to help the least of these my brothers and sisters, you were refusing to help me."
>
> Matthew 25:45

It saddens me to think that at times I have turned away from Jesus and refused to help his children. In doing so, I spurned him as well. Fortunately, God forgives us and each day is a new opportunity for us to serve his children. Perhaps it doesn't pay to "cry over spilt milk," but crying over spilt children can make all the difference in the world.

Let's cry over the lost children, and make sure they are found. God wants all of his children to experience the peace and joy that he planned for us. What a joy it is for us that we get to be God's loving hands in this world. We get to find his lost children and bring them back to him!

Dear Father,

Thank you for trusting us to take care of your children. We are sorry that we haven't cried more than we have over lost children. Please forgive us for our missed opportunities. Help us to recognize when your children need help and give us the wisdom and patience to work with them. Amen.

Where is the Gratitude?

How often are we thanked for what we do? My guess is not very often. We more than likely get a "thank you" now and then from colleagues. If we are lucky, we hear occasionally from our bosses that we are doing a good job. On rare occasions, parents may thank us for our efforts or tell our supervisors about our dedication and hard work. If we are really fortunate, we will hear from students years later that we made a real difference in their lives. This is hardly enough encouraging feedback for people who have totally dedicated their lives to helping others.

Humans are "fueled" by acknowledgment and praise. We need a "thank you" as much as a car needs gas. If we do not feel recognized or appreciated, we have a hard time getting revved up for the job! Unfortunately, it is not uncommon to see educators completely run out of gas and quit the profession.

I have heard it expressed that educators are like buckets of praise. Their job is to build children up by constantly showering them with praise and attention. Once educators' buckets have been emptied, they need to be refilled. What does it take to keep refilling these buckets? Portions of these buckets can be refilled with intrinsic positive self-worth. Educators who know they work hard and get good results can partially refill their own buckets. But what of the remaining portions of these buckets? If they must be refilled by praise from others, we could be in for a long wait.

Jesus tells us not to look for praise because we have only done our duty:

In the same way, when you obey me you should say, "We are not worthy of praise. We are servants who have simply done our duty."

Luke 17:10

If we are serving the Lord, we are not to waste time seeking praise from people. Praise from people is no longer necessary to keep our buckets full. God does this for us. God provides us with a bucket that never empties. We will never run out of energy as long as we serve God and his children!

Although we are not to seek praise for ourselves, we should spend time and effort building up those around us. Let's select some people with whom we work and praise them for serving others. Let's provide some fuel for our fellow educators. I find that the more I fill another person's bucket, the more fuel my bucket seems to have. It is rather like ordering the "bottomless bucket of fries" at one of my favorite restaurants; good things just keep coming!

Dear Father,

Thank you for providing us with a never-ending bucket of praise that nourishes our children and replenishes us. Please keep us refueled so that we may accomplish your will. Amen.

Matt Stephen, Ed.D.

In a Child's Shoes

Children have a different way of looking at life than adults. I discover this repeatedly. One of my first days on the job as an elementary school assistant principal (newly arrived from the high school world), a child came to me in tears. He said, "Mr. Stephen, Anthony cut me!" Looking for blood, I asked him where he was hurt. I soon found that the "cut" was someone getting in front of him in line. Another day at another school, a child came to the front office looking for the principal. One of the secretaries pointed to the principal of the school (a woman) and said, "There is the principal. She is right there." The little girl looked at her in frustration and said, "No, not her. I want the boy principal!" In addition, one day I got a love note from one of my students that said, "Dear Mr. Stephen, I love you for a principal...you make a good one for your age." I never lack for good stories that come from the eyes and mouths of the children. They certainly think differently than we do.

This difference in thinking, however, can create problems. For example, one of the toughest situations for educators who are trying to teach the three R's to students is that the students are more interested in the three F's: Food, Fun, and Friends. It is difficult to capture and maintain students' attention while they are focusing on the three F's. I once asked a fifth grade student what she would do if she were to become the principal. Her reply was that she would play music over the public announcement system, serve better food, and have more recess. I asked her about the curriculum and student performance on standardized tests, and she said that she would worry about that later.

Students have a tremendous need for the three F's. At times it seems they will go to any length to avoid the three R's in order to continue their search for food, fun, and friends. To fully understand their wants and needs, we must walk in their shoes. This is not easy because their shoes are too small, and it hurts to squeeze into those shoes. Getting inside of a child's mind also takes effort and can cause discomfort. As difficult as it is, we must get to know our students and tailor our instruction to their interests.

Jesus tells us the importance of understanding children and imitating them:

> Therefore, anyone who becomes as humble as this little child is the greatest in the Kingdom of Heaven.
> Matthew 18:4

Jesus tells us that there are great advantages to thinking like a child. By humbling ourselves and trying to understand his children, we are elevated in the kingdom of heaven!

Dear Father,

We are your children who are serving your children. Help us to love, protect, and understand your children as much as you love, protect, and understand us. Amen.

Be Quick to Listen

When someone comes to us with a problem, how do we react? While he or she is talking, do we ...

- Formulate the perfect answer?
- Think of advice that we can give?
- Interrupt before he/she finishes?
- Mentally go over our "To Do List?"
- Contemplate our own problems?
- Daydream about something else?

Unfortunately, these are some normal actions that we often take as we attempt to listen to other people. I can recall times when I was listening to someone and suddenly realized that I had not heard a thing that he or she said. I found that embarrassing because I was signaling to that person that his or her situation was not important to me.

Jesus summed up the importance of listening to others by saying:

> You must be compassionate, just as your Father is compassionate.
>
> Luke 6:36

We are told to be compassionate with others just as God is compassionate with us. We demonstrate our compassion for others through our attentiveness. Hearing someone is easy. Listening to someone is difficult. When we truly listen, we tune into feelings as well as words. In a way, we listen with our hearts as well as our ears. We can best listen to a person by climbing into his or her shoes and walking around in them for a while.

One day a student asked me what I do all day as a principal. I thought for a moment and said, "I talk and listen all day long." In a nutshell, that is what educators do—we communicate. Listening is far more important than talking when it comes to effective communication. We have all found that students and parents want more than being told what to do. They want to be heard as well. We are given excellent advice on how to interact with others from James:

> My dear brothers and sisters, be quick to listen, slow to speak, and slow to get angry. Your anger can never make things right in God's sight.
>
> James 1: 19–20

What great advice this is! Be quick to listen and slow to anger. Arguments would be impossible if everyone concentrated on listening rather than talking. Imagine what our schools would be like if every person (students, staff, and parents) made a special effort to listen to others and not get angry. Schools would truly be heaven on earth!

Dear Father,

Remind us that listening is far better than talking. We often forget this. Help us to be quick to listen and slow to anger so that we may pass this on to your children. Amen.

Matt Stephen, Ed.D.

In the Eyes of the Beholder

Children watch us very closely. Every move we make is a model for them to see. Children are formulating their personalities and the guiding principles they will live by for the rest of their lives, and they are learning from our examples every day. What tremendous pressure that puts on us! Since children are using our lives as patterns for their own, we must lead near-perfect lives. How can we do that? We cannot be perfect, so what is the most important quality for us to model?

Peter tells us what he believes should be our focal point:

> Most important of all, continue to show deep love for each other, for love covers a multitude of sins.
>
> 1 Peter 4:8

Peter tells us that love binds and blinds! It is great to know that if we concentrate on showing love for others, this will cover up a multitude of sins. We certainly are not perfect; however, people do not notice all of our faults because they know that we love and care for them. This holds true in our professional and personal lives. I know that I benefit from this more than most people. I love my wife and kids with a passion, so they do not see the many, many flaws I possess. They are quick to forgive and forget because they know I love them. In my professional life, I do my best to show love and care for the people with whom I work. Those people who believe that I love and care for them are quick to forgive me when I slip and fall.

Those who do not feel the love and care are much more critical of my leadership.

Our students hold us in high regard in spite of our numerous faults. It is good that our loving attitudes are able to cloak our faults in the eyes of our students! Think of a teacher that you appreciated as you were growing up. Think of all the reasons you liked this teacher. Now think of this teacher's faults. Most likely, you cannot think of many. As students, we overlooked many of our teachers' faults because we were loved by them!

Our relationships with our peers work the same way. We are mature and aware enough to know that our colleagues are not perfect. However, we tend to overlook the sins of one another if we believe that we are loved. It is love that holds us together and keeps us working cooperatively.

Dear Father,

Thank you for the love that binds and blinds. Please help us to demonstrate this love to those around us. Amen.

Matt Stephen, Ed.D.

Sacrifice

Serving children in schools comes with a tremendous cost. Often, we have to make great personal sacrifices. We spend long days on the job, we miss special events with our families, and we give up personal time and pleasures. We dedicate so much of ourselves to the job that we think of the job even during our personal time. We are not allowed to let go of the job mentally. Lesson planning, student assessment, instructional modifications, and student behavior weigh heavily on our minds. We are on duty twenty-four hours a day, seven days a week. Eventually, we feel drained and depleted with very little energy left for ourselves.

We are told that those who sacrifice for others are rewarded:

> Feed the hungry and help those in trouble. Then your light will shine out from the darkness, and the darkness around you will be as bright as day. The Lord will guide you continually, watering your life when you are dry and keeping you healthy, too. You will be like a well-watered garden, like an ever-flowing spring.
>
> Isaiah 58:10–11

We pay a heavy price for choosing to serve children, but we can take heart because God sees and rewards our efforts. We are told that God will bless our lives by guiding us and keeping us healthy so we can continue to serve him. Because God has chosen us to lead his children, we should always be ready to sacrifice ourselves and be confident that God will take care of us.

Sometimes our dedication to others comes at the highest possible cost. For example, Shannon Wright, a middle school teacher in Jonesboro, Arkansas, gave her life for one of her students. One day a mentally deranged student opened fire on fellow students on a middle school playground. Shannon Wright shielded one of her students from that sniper's bullets. Jesus tells us that there is no greater love than personal sacrifice:

> The greatest love is shown when people lay down their lives for their friends.
>
> John 15:13

The greatest love is to be willing to lay down our lives for the benefit of others. Rarely do teachers literally give up their lives for their children as Shannon Wright did; but we do make many personal sacrifices for our students every day. Thankfully, God has our backs. He will ensure that we are an ever-flowing spring because we are serving his children. Let's live for today, and let's enjoy our call to lead others. Through our sacrifices for others, we brighten the world for our children with God's light.

Dear Father,

As you sacrificed for me, let me be a sacrifice for your children. Thank you for using me to light the world for your children. Amen

Don't Drive Into the Smoke

Once while driving through Oklahoma, I saw road signs that said, "Don't Drive into the Smoke." I had never seen this sign before, and I was puzzled. I soon realized that grass fires must be somewhat common in Oklahoma, and the signs are reminding motorists of the hazards of driving through the near-zero visibility of smoke. I could not help but chuckle because these signs were dedicated to stating the obvious. Why don't we have signs that say: "Don't Drive into the Fire," or "Don't Drive into Brick Walls," or "Don't Drive Off of the Cliff?" Obvious advice can sound funny - especially if it is posted on road signs!

We are given obvious advice from people throughout our lives. Some advice we listen to, some we do not. People who are risk-takers do not always follow everyone's obvious advice. They strike out on their own against all odds. These bold actions call for great faith in self, others, and God. In order for us to have great faith, we need to feel that we are not alone or unprotected. David sang long ago about the Lord's protection:

> But you, O Lord, are a shield around me, my glory,
> and the one who lifts my head high.
>
> Psalm 3:3

David should know about God's protection. After all, he slew the giant, Goliath, with a small stone and a sling. He tells us that God will shield us and lift us up when we are taking risks. As educators, we often avoid taking risks for fear of failure, ridicule, or retaliation. We feel more secure if we stand back and watch the brave ones stick their necks out. The Bible tells us repeatedly that God's protection is limitless. If we work within God's will, we do not need to worry about taking risks. We can be confident that with God's help our successes will be greater than expected.

Christopher Columbus was a risk-taker. He challenged the odds and sailed into the unknown to find a new trade route to the Indies. I am sure many people thought him crazy and headed for a terrible demise, but Columbus had faith in God and in himself. God rewarded him for his faith and risk-taking. God blessed him by allowing him to discover a new world!

A new world is out there waiting for our students. We are blessed to be given the opportunity to lead them through our school system and prepare them to take risks to attain big rewards. We can model for our students our reliance upon God for his protection as we take risks.

Dear Father,

You are our strength and our shield. Thank you for the protection that frees our minds from worry. Help us to take risks, conquer this world, and lead your children to their best possible future. Amen.

Matt Stephen, Ed.D.

Listen to God

When and where do you do your best thinking? Do you do your best thinking alone or in a group ... morning or night ... quiet or busy places? I once did my best thinking in the shower. It was quiet, steamy, warm, and comfortable in my shower. Given time, I could solve problems, formulate new ideas, and set the agenda for the day. If I had been able to procure a waterproof pen and paper, I could have stayed in the shower longer and solved the problems of the entire world. My wife put an end to this style of thinking because of the water and electric bills.

I propose that we can do our best thinking in meditative silence. Screening out the world and its problems is necessary when focusing on problem solving or planning for the future. Before we can focus on the big picture, we have to empty our minds of the trivial pursuits that distract us.

I hear God when I am silent. He speaks to me in solitude. It is my responsibility to arrange this quiet time for meditation. If I do not arrange for this personal time with God, I am choosing not to listen to what he has to say. This is when things begin to go wrong for me. When I listen only to myself or rely upon my own abilities, I am cutting out the greatest help that exists. God is always with us and ready to help, but we must call upon him. God's answer on how to meditate is the simplest of all:

Be silent, and know that I am God!

Psalm 46:10

This is one of the shortest and most powerful verses in the Bible. Notice that God did not say, "Try to slow down and be relatively convinced that I am God." He tells us that if we stop and give him our complete attention, we will know beyond any doubt that he is God. This will open a communion with God and allow us to strengthen our personal relationship with him. Inspiration from God will come through this quiet meditation. We can take time to block out the world and listen in silence. If we do, God's help will come in loud and clear.

Dear Father,

Help us to seek solitude and listen to you. We need your inspiration in order to best serve your children. Amen.

December

December is definitely a unique month. It signifies the end or near end of the semester. It holds one of the most celebrated and joyous of holidays. It also provides a rest for educators in the form of a mid-year or winter vacation. We take time for our families and ourselves during this break from work. A spirit of loving, giving, and sharing pervades our thinking. Our traditions and celebrations provide us with a distraction from the everyday occurrences of our school life.

This month also marks the first day of winter. The cold weather and possibility of snow sparks thoughts of roasting chestnuts, hot chocolate, carolers, silver bells, and sleigh rides. Once again, family takes over in our thoughts and actions. This month also includes frantic decorating, attending numerous parties, and last minute gift buying on Christmas Eve before the stores close.

Even though family and friends take much of our attention this month, we cannot forget our students and colleagues. We can ask those around us how they are doing and stick around to listen to their answer. We can be there if they need to talk. We can walk in their shoes and feel their situations. We can cry over our unlovable children and see them through God's eyes. We are here to serve all of God's children—not just the easy ones.

A hectic, frantic pace followed by peaceful, blissful, cheerful relaxation is the oxymoron called "December." Take time to celebrate good will with your students before Christmas Break. Indulge yourself and your family during this wonderful season. Most of all, we can remember the true reason behind the season: God's greatest gift, Jesus Christ, God's only son our Lord.

Matt Stephen, Ed.D.

I'm Tired of Being Good!

In December 1998, I had a very interesting conversation with a first grader. The little boy said to me, "I wish Christmas would be over soon!" I asked him why he felt that way and he said, "Because I'm tired of being good!"

Isn't this an interesting dilemma for children around Christmas time? Kids think that two weeks of good behavior before Christmas will counteract the fifty previous weeks of questionable behavior. Even a mere two weeks of good behavior can be exhausting for them. Since this conversation, I have realized that this is true for adults as well. We can also get tired of being good. It is hard work for adults to maintain good behavior day after day after day.

Educators can tire of always being a role model for others and the constant expectation of being on one's best behavior. We get tired of always striving to be patient, understanding, polite, diplomatic, reserved, friendly, supportive, empathetic, nice, and humble. It seems that leaders are expected to exhibit an extra degree of "goodness" around the clock each day, and this is tough to do!

Christian leadership calls for constant Christ-like behavior, but it does not always come naturally or easily. Sometimes it seems that leaning toward being bad is a more natural way of behaving, and we have to consciously force ourselves to be good. We must ask for God's strength and patience each day. We are told never to give up on being good:

> So don't get tired of doing what is good. Don't get discouraged and give up, for we will reap a harvest

of blessing at the appropriate time. Whenever we have the opportunity, we should do good to everyone, especially to our Christian brothers and sisters.

Galatians 6:9–10

The reward for being good in God's eyes is awesome! We will reap the "harvest of blessing" some day when we stand face-to-face with our loving Father. The anticipation of this eternal reward should be enough to refuel our goodness when we feel ourselves running low, and our students will be blessed through our examples of never-ending goodness!

Dear Father,

Although the process of being on my best behavior tires me at times, I always want to walk within your will. Please give me the strength and endurance I need to continuously strive for your perfection. Amen.

Matt Stephen, Ed.D.

Here to Serve

I remember years ago a phone company advertised itself as "The Only Phone Company in Town, but We Try Not to Act Like It." I always wondered if that was true. The horror of the consumer world is that companies will gain monopolies, inflate prices, and reduce quality of service. With no competition, consumers would be totally at their mercy.

I wonder if some educational systems might have this nightmare of an attitude: "Since we are the only public school system in town, we do not need to worry about customer satisfaction. If the students and parents are unhappy, it is too bad because we have always done it this way and we are not going to change." This kind of attitude is far from a service attitude. It is an attitude of arrogance and indifference.

In the consumer world, attitudes like this would run companies straight out of business. School districts, however, are funded by tax dollars and run by a small group of people often in the form of a school board. Customers do not have the privilege of switching school districts if they become dissatisfied because they are tied to the location where they pay their taxes. Basically, school districts have a captive audience of customers. So why should educators worry about running off customers? We must still concern ourselves with customer satisfaction because when we lose a customer, we turn a student away from learning and the opportunity to reap the long-term benefits of a good education. We do not go out of business, but we can ruin someone's life.

We cannot afford to exhibit arrogance or indifference as we work with our children and their parents. We can exhibit an attitude of service. We can be genuinely humble. Service must be in our hearts and minds. A service attitude will help us to gain the trust of our children and their parents. Then perhaps, they will honor us for the service that we perform. The joy of serving others is ours, and no one can take that away.

Jesus tells us how important a service attitude is:

> And whoever wants to be the first must be the slave of all. For even I, the Son of Man, came here not to be served but to serve others, and to give my life as a ransom for many.
>
> Mark 10:44–45

There is no doubt that we are expected to serve one another here on earth. Moreover, we are to humbly serve one another. Jesus told us of the dangers of honoring ourselves and the rewards of humbleness:

> For the proud will be humbled, but the humble will be honored.
>
> Luke 14:11

Jesus Christ provided the perfect example of what true service is. He humbled himself as he served us here on earth, even to the point of total self-sacrifice. His charge to us is to become as Christ-like as possible. We are to humbly serve others to the best of our ability, even to the point of self-sacrifice. The education profession provides us an excellent vehicle in which to humbly serve God and his children.

Dear Father,

Thank you for leading us to the profession in which we can make a great difference in your children's futures. Help us to maintain a service attitude as we educate your children. Please grant us the strength to be humble toward others; and as we are aware of your sacrifice for us, help us to sacrifice ourselves for others. Amen.

Stoplights of Life

I have grown accustomed to waiting a few seconds before I enter an intersection after the light turns green. Often, someone will run a red light by a full three seconds or more. This doesn't sound like much, but it is a fatal accident waiting to happen. It is hard for me to imagine someone so selfish or in enough of a hurry to risk a possible collision in the middle of an intersection just to save thirty seconds.

Our society as a whole is slowly losing its stoplights. People seem more likely to disobey laws today than ever before. As a result, the honest citizens are penalized for the acts of the dishonest ones. For example, we have to pay for gas up front and we have to show identification to write a check or use a credit card because of other people's dishonesty. Also, anger seems to be at an all-time high. Some people have lost their inner-stoplights that control their anger responses. As a result, we see personal violence on the rise. It appears that we are creating a very scary world for our children to inherit.

As servant leaders, we can stand up for what is right and fair. We can speak our minds and show the courage to do what is right. We owe it to the next generation to build a better world for tomorrow. We are in an excellent position to teach our nation's children about life's stoplights. We can show them that there are certain boundaries that cannot be crossed without dire consequences. We can also model and teach self-control and self-responsibility to our children. We can teach them to stand up for what is right.

Jesus tells us of the rewards for standing up for what is right:

Matt Stephen, Ed.D.

By standing firm, you will win your souls.

Luke 21:19

With God's help, we can stand up and do what is right. Our real struggle in life is not against people. It is against the evil that people do. With God's strength and protection, we can win our battles for preserving our stoplights. Our payoff for standing firm is a better life on earth and an eternal life with God for our children and ourselves.

Dear Father,

With your help, we can fight the evil that is taking over our world. Help us to stand up and make this a better place for your children. Amen.

Be a Shining Light

Do educators add to the doom and gloom of society? Unfortunately, we do in a way. It is easy to get caught up in the negativism that pervades our world today. Isn't it easy to listen to someone who is spreading some really juicy gossip or get caught up in the fun of lambasting parents who do not raise their children as we would approve? Do we find ourselves criticizing students in front of other educators? Have we ever wished for Friday on a Monday?

All of us display negative attitudes at one time or another. Negative thoughts seem to arise easily and naturally. However, negativity can lead to our destruction. The more negative thoughts that invade our lives, the more sour we become. I heard once that a grumpy old person is created one thought at a time! We even wear our negative thoughts on our faces in the form of scowls, frowns, and "poor pitiful me" expressions.

Positive thoughts, on the other hand, tend to lighten one's life. It is actually documented that positive thoughts can lighten and cheer one's face. Is there joy in our faces? Do our faces radiate with the love of God? Are we serving as a shining light to guide others along the correct path in life?

Paul tells us to stay away from complaining and arguing and to be a light shining in a dark world:

> In everything you do, stay away from complaining and arguing, so that no one can speak a word of blame against you. You are to live clean, innocent lives as children of God in a dark world full of

Matt Stephen, Ed.D.

crooked and perverse people. Let your lives shine
brightly before them.

Philippians 2:14–15

God tells us to focus on the joys of life. We can look for
the joys that surround us. We can fill our minds with
positive thoughts and allow them to illuminate our faces
and our entire lives. Other people want us to be negative.
They want us to join them in their pitiful, negative world.
The next time someone tries to pull us down with them
into a negative conversation, we can say, "No thanks, I am
trying to cut down!"

Dear Father,
  Thank you for your unconditional love. We are your
lights in this world. Please help us shine our lights for others
so they can also find you and your infinite love. Amen.

The Biggest Picture

We are often criticized because we do not see the big picture. Principals complain because teachers and school staff focus only on their individual classrooms, grade levels, or subject areas. Superintendents and central office staff complain that principals focus only on their buildings and their students. State leaders complain that school superintendents think only of their school districts. Each level of the bureaucracy accuses the next level of having tunnel vision.

We can all admit that at times we are guilty of tunnel vision; and tunnel vision is not all bad. An intense, unshakable focus can help us to quickly solve problems in times of crisis. The downside of tunnel vision occurs when we have such great concern for our own corner of the world that we do not see the big picture in which we are a subset. We might find ourselves saying things like: "They don't care about us because we are just little people," or "They are too busy to be concerned about us," or "They don't understand or have forgotten what it is really like." We can be quite hurt if we feel isolated or unimportant to someone else.

Paul tells us that it is important to work together:

> Then make me truly happy by agreeing whole-heartedly with each other, loving one another, and working together with one heart and purpose.
> Philippians 2:2

We need to step away from our individual situations and see how everyone works together to create the big

Matt Stephen, Ed.D.

picture. At the school level, each employee has individual concerns and challenges, but everyone works together for the children. At the district level, we can see how all local schools work together to prepare children for entering the community as productive adult citizens. The next step is to see the bigger picture of national education. This involves the intellectual, emotional, spiritual, behavioral, and social growth of our entire nation. If educators work together with one heart, mind, and purpose, our states can produce a new generation that will strengthen our nation.

We are now ready to see the biggest picture in education. We are preparing our children to live their lives as God intends. We are creating a godlier nation here on earth and ensuring eternal life for ourselves and our children. This is the most important, lasting education that we can give our children.

Dear Father,

Help us to focus on the biggest picture in education, which is to share your love and lead others to you. Together we in education can work with one heart, mind, and purpose for your children. Amen.

Turn Your Creative Juices Loose

I wonder if you are also guilty of my mistake. I nearly killed my creative side. I discovered my creative side in high school. I enjoyed many adventures and spent hours writing poetry and playing music on oboe and clarinet. I graduated high school and put my "toys" away. I then become very good at studying and making good grades. After college, I become very good at working. At age twenty-four, I prematurely become forty-something. I threw myself into the professional world and began climbing the corporate ladder. I took work home every night and on weekends. I graded papers and planned lessons with my free time. I attended graduate school at night and during the summers. I also worked extra jobs to help pay for school. I forgot how to be creative and enjoy the beauty of the world! Recently, I have begun playing the oboe and writing poetry again, and I am happier for it. I look forward to the times that I get to retreat from work and create music and poetry.

We all have a creative side, and I dare say some of us never discover it. Is it possible that the world's greatest writer, artist, thespian, or musician will never be discovered because we are covered up in work? God wants us to be creative. He has given each of us the ability to create beauty. If we will take the time, we can generate beauty for this world in a number of ways. We need to be creative so we can change the normal everyday work pattern that we have set for ourselves.

Each of us has a creative side, and we can create beauty for others to enjoy. When was the last time we let our

Matt Stephen, Ed.D.

creative selves loose? Have we buried our talents in favor of working? How creative are we at work? Do we ever allow our creativity to produce change in our professional lives?

God tells us to use the creative talents that he gave us:

> God has given gifts to each of you from his great variety of spiritual gifts. Manage them well so that God's generosity can flow through you.
>
> 1 Peter 4:10

We can each find something to pursue with a passion—something that will rekindle our creative spirit. There is no rule that says we cannot be creative at work. In fact, when we are creative at school, we are providing a great role model for our students. We are telling them that we will use our God-given gifts. If we urge our students to use their God-given talents, we will discover our new super stars!

Dear Father,

Thank you for our creative side. Help us not to lock away our creativity in order to save more time for work. Amen.

The Week before Christmas Break:
In an Elementary School in Texas

It was the week before Christmas Break,
Monday morning, 7:03.
Not a person was stirring,
except our before school program, latchkey.

The staff soon would be braced at their stations,
their hearts filled with excitement (and a little dread),
of the endless activities, wild children, and extra paperwork,
that they expected in the week ahead.

Sitting alone at my desk,
I must admit that I also did try
to wish that this week
had already gone by.

When suddenly from the office I heard such a clatter,
I sprang to the door to see what was the matter.
I saw a gentleman signing for a visitor's badge so quick,
I knew in a moment it must be St. Nick.

It was two weeks shy of Christmas, so I asked
"Santa, what are you doing here?"
To which he turned and smiled and said,
"I've come to spread some news of good cheer."

Matt Stephen, Ed.D.

He said, "You need a reminder
I can't stress enough.
You spend too much time
sweating the little stuff!"

"This week will be hectic, it is true,
but treasure each moment as it happens to you.
For amidst all of the usual toil and strife,
you have a chance to make a difference in a life."

"Don't forget the true meaning of Christmas,
a reminder of God's gift from above–
the gift of his Son,
and his never-ending love."

"This love is to be shared,
not hoarded inside.
You must wrap your children in it
with your arms open wide."

Before I could respond,
he dashed out to the hall
saying, "Merry Christmas, Happy New Year,
and God bless y'all!"

Isn't it ironic that we educators get wound up so tight during the Christmas season? It is a time of year that we are supposed to feel a special peace and good will toward others, yet we are about to get on one another's last nerve. The combination of too much to do, our own fatigue, and excited children can send our Christmas cheer into a downward spiral! Only a focus on the true meaning of Christmas can pull us out of this pre-Christmas nosedive:

> The angel reassured them, "Don't be afraid!" he said. "I bring you good news of great joy for everyone! The Savior—yes, the Messiah, the Lord—has been born tonight in Bethlehem, the city of David!"
>
> Luke 2:10–11

Dear Father,

This is a blessed season. Thank you for the birth of Jesus, his sacrifice, and your gift of everlasting life. Please help us to focus on your gifts and not to fret over trivial things. Amen.

January

January is a time for new beginnings. We celebrate the beginning of a new year through resolutions and rededication. We make resolutions for our personal and professional lives, and we rededicate ourselves to our ideals and to our students. It is a time to review our personal goals for the year and make necessary adjustments. It is also time to have the students reflect on their accomplishments and communicate their progress to their parents.

We are refreshed from our vacation and ready for the second half of the school year. As we begin a new semester, we again find ourselves planning curriculum scope and sequence and instructional strategies. We may have picked up a new subject to teach or our supervisors may have given us new responsibilities to handle. We are gaining new students who need to be acclimated to our rules and routines. In many ways, we are starting all over again. God provides great help when it comes to new beginnings. We are privileged to go to him and for his wisdom, strength, and peace.

January is a month to focus on our cultural diversity here in America. We celebrate our diversity through special events such as the Martin Luther King Day and World Religion Day. Opportunities are provided to help us understand that although we are different and unique individuals, we are interdependent upon one another. Also, we celebrate our school nurses on National School Nurse Day. We have a chance to thank our "Angels of Mercy" for the life-saving services they provide for our children.

Post-Christmas Vacation Blues

Every year I am struck with the "Post-Christmas Vacation Blues." My thoughts are, "I can't believe that these two weeks went by so quickly, and I have to go back to work on Monday." However, after deep contemplation, I always realize that I am glad to go back to work after all. Here are the top ten reasons:

1. I have run out of Christmas money and the month of January is already looking quite lean.

2. I have opened up all of my presents and it does not look like I am getting any more.

3. I have to begin proving to Santa that I deserve a visit from him next Christmas Eve.

4. I cannot afford to totally quit working. My family has this silly habit of requiring food and shelter.

5. I miss being surrounded by talented and caring colleagues.

6. I miss the adoration of the students. My own kids know me too well to adore me.

7. The list of chores at home was getting too long, and I was running out of excuses as to why I could not get to them.

8. I cannot wait to see the new projects I will receive from my bosses.

9. I cannot wait to see what our legislature will do to us.

10. My wife needs a break.

Seriously, the true reason that we are glad to be back at work is that we have a mission to serve others. The two-week vacation gives us an opportunity to rest, visit with friends and relatives, and do some chores. It is a very self-serving two weeks (which we need), but we are ready to begin serving our children again.

Paul reminds us why we work:

> Remember that the Lord will give you an inheritance as your reward, and the Master you are serving is Christ.
>
> Colossians 3:24

Our Lord is our true boss. He is the one we are working for and trying to please. We, as educators, have dedicated ourselves to serving God's children. The two-week rest is nice, but we must get back to our calling. Together, let's renew that service spirit that keeps us coming back for more!

Dear Father,

Thank you for the rest. You are our shelter and our shield. Renew us and prepare us to lead your children according to your will. Amen.

New Year's Resolutions

We do not need to generate a New Year's Resolutions list for this year. We will not need to go through the painful process of self-reflection and generating numerous resolutions that we may or may not keep. Paul has done the thinking for all of us. Since we are chosen by God, Paul says that we must take on the following characteristics:

- compassion,
- kindness,
- humility,
- patience,
- gentleness,
- forgiveness,
- love,
- peace, and
- thankfulness.

These characteristics come from Colossians 3:12–15. Since these are the character traits that the Lord wants us to exhibit, all other resolutions seem to pale in importance. However, these characteristics are not easy to exhibit on a constant basis. These traits are especially vulnerable when we are in a hurry. Because these are deliberate actions, we have to engage conscious thought and take extra time to demonstrate these traits. When pressed for time, it is easier to overlook these actions for the sake of speed and efficiency.

It is possible to slow down and live according to these characteristics both at home and at work. By demonstrating these traits at work, we are telling others how important living within God's will is to us. Jesus tells us his expectations for our character:

> You are to be perfect, even as your Father in heaven is perfect.
>
> Matthew 5:48

Perfection! Jesus tells us that we are to strive for perfection. This is no small order. As we strive for perfection, we must take the time to exhibit these characteristics outlined in Colossians. This resolution will cost us much time and effort, but the payoff will be enormous. If we follow this resolution, we stand to win our students because they crave this kind of attention from us.

Dear Father,

Thank you for choosing us to be your servants here on earth. Thank you for entrusting us with your children. Please help us as we daily strive for perfection. Help us to slow down and make these traits a natural part of our character. In this way, we can show others how important you are to us. Amen.

Matt Stephen, Ed.D.

Shelter in a Storm

Picture yourself as a warm, cozy room with a fireplace and that some of your students are wandering outside on a very cold night. You serve as a refuge—a place to step into from the dark and bitter cold. You are a place where children can warm themselves, regenerate, and feel safe for a while.

Some of our children spend their lives in a cold, hard environment. They go through some tough times, and they may begin to wonder if there is any purpose to life. At times, they will seek refuge and may need to step into your cozy room for a while. You can warm them up and make them feel better about themselves and the world.

From Student to Teacher:
A Love Poem

There is a room of which I know
that always has a fire aglow.
In it sits a chair all plush.
The sounds within are all a hush.

There are blankets to make me cozy and warm
and a bolted door to keep out harm.
The book on the table contains a happy ending.
It makes my time well-worth spending.

There is a cup of hot chocolate by the chair,
and the smell of fresh baked bread in the air.
How long I stay, I need not worry
because time slows down, there is no hurry.

This room is in my mind.
the times I enter it are few.
I am mostly in this room I find
when I am close to you.

Our Lord serves as our refuge. As Moses told us:

> The eternal God is your refuge, and his everlasting
> arms are under you.
>
> Deuteronomy 33:27

Jesus tells us that we are to shelter our children:

> And anyone who welcomes a little child like this
> on my behalf, is welcoming me.
>
> Matthew 18:5

Just as God serves as our refuge, we are to serve as protectors of his children. Jesus tells us that as we serve his children, we are also serving him. As educators, we are in the perfect position to serve as a refuge for our students.

Dear Father,
Thank you for protecting us and serving as our refuge. Please continue to strengthen us to do the same for your children. Amen.

The Proper Focus

What do you surround yourself with on a daily basis to remind you of God and his will for your life? Do you hang inspirational posters on the wall or keep inspirational literature at arms length? We all know that it is difficult in a public school setting to surround ourselves with items that remind us of God's plan ... or is it?

I knew a principal who kept a Bible right in the middle of his conference table. I have seen teachers' rooms with Biblical sayings posted and pictures on the wall that reminded me of God and his beautiful world. I have a poster of the fruits of the spirit on my wall and pictures of lighthouses filling my office. Lighthouses remind me of my true purpose—to be a shining light for God's children. Many discreet items such as these help keep my heart and mind on God and his will while I am at work.

Focus on God? Sure, Sundays are easy! We meet with other godly people and focus on God and his plan for our lives and our world. But weekdays are different. We can find ourselves in secular settings with some very ungodly people. There are times when we feel that we are far away from God's peace, and we need a support system to lean on throughout the week. During the week, we can feel ourselves losing God's peace as we fret over the ways of the world. We can "reel ourselves in" and regain God's peace by surrounding ourselves with symbols that remind us of God's presence. If we haven't done so already, we can find our symbolic rock to hold onto such as a visual Bible verse, a picture on the wall, a song, or a friend.

We are told of the eternal advantages of the right focus:

So we don't look at the troubles we can see right now; rather, we look forward to what we have not yet seen. For the troubles we see will soon be over, but the joys to come will last forever.

2 Corinthians 4:18

As humans, we need immediate rewards. Paul tells us there are immediate, earthly rewards for the correct focus:

But when the Holy Spirit controls our lives, he will produce this kind of fruit in us: love, joy, peace, patience, kindness, goodness, faithfulness, gentleness and self-control.

Galatians 5:22

Here on earth, we can enjoy God's peace and other fruits of the spirit if our focus is on him. Do others know that you believe in God and trust in him? Can they tell by your focus, your action, your sense of peace? Our profession gives us the perfect stage to share our heavenly focus with others throughout the week.

Dear Father,

Thank you for your fruits of the spirit. Without them, we would surely feel lost. Help us to focus on you and your will throughout the week as well as on Sundays. Amen.

Matt Stephen, Ed.D.

Laying Lives Aside

I have often wondered what some of my teachers would have done had they not been public school teachers. Many of them were brilliant in their subjects, and I believe that they could have been celebrities in their respective fields. I do not doubt that some of them sacrificed great wealth and prestige to teach in public schools. I cannot help but wonder what they gave up in order to be there for my classmates and me. I wish that I had shown more appreciation toward my teachers as I traveled through my junior high and high school years.

John tells us how much we should be willing to give to others:

> We know what real love is because Christ gave up his life for us. And so we also ought to give up our lives for our Christian brothers and sisters.
>
> 1 John 3:16

Although most of us do not give up our physical lives for others, we often lay our personal lives aside. We take time away from our families and friends in order to do our best for our students. We spend a good deal of time attending workshops, seminars, and college courses to make ourselves more effective at our jobs. We work many hours outside of the normal workday. We plan and assess on our own time because we are constantly attending to our students' immediate needs during school hours.

We often give up our own wants and pursuits in order to teach in public schools. Let's face it; we are not paid what we deserve. We could be making more money in almost any other profession, so apparently we are not in the teaching profession for the high salaries. As servant leaders, we know that God expects us to give up ourselves for the benefit of others. This means considering others' wants and needs before our own. We have mastered selflessness; as educators, we do this every day. We have chosen to follow our calling—to serve God and his children.

Dear Father,

We thank you for your example of selfless sacrifice. Help us to focus on your children as we make our living sacrifice to you. Although we are not rich by earthly standards, we are building up our heavenly wealth by serving your children. Amen.

No Middle Ground

Are there teachers in your past that you cannot remember? Are there teachers that you will remember for the rest of your life? I propose that the teachers we remember well are those teachers who left either a very loving, positive memory in our heads or a sour taste in our mouths. Perhaps the teachers whom we cannot remember very well are those who left a very slight impression on our memories due to the minimal personal interactions that took place.

As educators in schools, we work with our students seven hours a day, five days a week. Children are highly impressionable and vulnerable, and they are formulating their outlook on life while in our schools; so how can we not make some kind of an impression on their lives? I believe that there is no middle ground in teacher-student relationships. We are either a positive or a negative influence upon our children; it is impossible to leave a neutral influence. An educator who chooses to have minimal or no personal interactions with his or her students (an attitude of indifference) is choosing to leave a negative influence. As servant leaders, it is our duty to care for all of our students and show them that they are important. It is our duty to leave a positive, lasting impression. To do anything less is a disservice to our children.

Paul tells us to take time to love one another:

> Knowing God leads to self-control. Self-control leads to patient endurance, and patient endurance leads to godliness. Godliness leads to love for

other Christians, and finally you will grow to have genuine love for everyone.

2 Peter 1:6–7

Jesus took time to visit with some of the most unpopular people of his time. He was often criticized for this. He took the time to let everyone know that they were important to him. Jesus tells us that how we treat others is important to him. How we interact with our children is also how we interact with Christ. This week let's take our most unlovable, undisciplined children aside and talk to them. Let's show them that we care about them and that they are important to us. All children are looking for someone who believes in them or at least cares enough to try. It may not work the first time, but persistence is the key.

Jesus also tells us often about the gift of eternal life. We are privileged to share love with one another here on earth, and our lives are blessed through the joy of loving and serving others. Best of all, the reward for this service is a blissful, eternal life with God. What a bargain!

Dear Father,

Thank you for the gift of eternal life in heaven with you. Help us to share that good news and joy with others. Give us the wisdom to know what to say and do for those who need our attention. Help us to take the time to build a relationship with each one of our students. Amen

Matt Stephen, Ed.D.

Bottom Line

I always tell my students that the bottom line to excellent behavior is doing the right thing even when adults are not looking. Our children can be masters at doing the right thing when under close supervision and behaving as if all rules are off when on their own. Some children carry this behavior into adulthood. For proof of this, just watch adult motorists speed up and slow down around police cars on the road. Once we see people do the right thing when others aren't looking, we know that they have internalized the right behavior.

Jesus gave us a bottom line many years ago:

> Then these righteous ones will reply, "Lord, when did we ever see you hungry and feed you? Or thirsty and give you something to drink? Or a stranger and show you hospitality? Or naked and give you clothing? When did we ever see you sick or in prison, and visit you?" And the King will tell them, "I assure you, when you did it to one of these least of these my brothers and sisters, you were doing it to me!"
>
> Matthew 25:37–40

Jesus's bottom line is for us to treat others right even when the authorities are not looking. Jesus tells us that when we are good to others, we are being good to him. Treating other people right is easy to do when they are "easy" people. Easy people are the people who are cooperative, friendly, and loving. Examples of easy people are friendly co-workers, church colleagues, friends, and family members. It is not as easy to treat difficult people right. These are the people who are high maintenance, troublemakers, or evil-spirited. By just being around us, they can drain our positive energy!

As servant leaders, we can model godly behavior constantly. We can treat other people (easy and difficult) right because Jesus tells us to do so - not because we are afraid of the consequences imposed by those in authority. The bottom line is that Jesus is always watching us, and he is our authority.

Dear Father,

I am sorry for mistreating others. When I do not treat others right, I make a mockery of your love. In the heat of the moment, help me to remember that when I show love for others, I am showing love for you. Amen.

Matt Stephen, Ed.D.

Career Check-up

After we have been in the education business for a few years, we reach a check-up point in our career. At this time, we examine our motives and accomplishments. We reflect upon our careers and ask some questions of ourselves:

- "Are we still working to achieve our goals and our dreams, or are we merely earning a paycheck?"
- "Are we providing a valuable service to others?"
- "Are we utilizing our God-given talents to help others?"

The realization that we are still striving to meet our calling leads to career satisfaction, and it is this satisfaction that leads to daily joy on the job.

God's counsel makes all the difference when evaluating one's career. I have changed directions many times in my career. I moved from classroom teacher to counselor to assistant principal to principal to university director to assistant superintendent and to university professor. I have enjoyed each position which I have held, but I wonder if all of the changes were truly necessary. As I reflect upon my many moves, I realize that some of my moves were more successful than others. I have to wonder how often God looked down upon me and said, "There he goes again, I wish he had consulted with me first." Perhaps I could have saved myself some trouble if I had truly attempted to follow God's will rather than try to meet my own wants and desires.

Are we happy and content with our lives? If not, what is it we truly want to do? If we are not already doing it, what is holding us back? It is hard to strike out on one's own and try something different, but it is sometimes necessary for one's happiness. I believe that God changes our direction by causing us to feel dissatisfied with our present situation. He speaks to us through our own discomfort. If we are unhappy with life the way it is, we can talk to God. He is waiting to hear from us.

Jesus tells us that God already knows what we think and feel:

> Your Father knows exactly what you need even before you ask him!
>
> Matthew 6: 8

We need to ask for God's counsel as we reflect upon our accomplishments and determine our goals for the future. In order to stay on the correct path, we should seek God's will for our lives. Living outside of his will only leads to confusion and unhappiness. He directs our lives, and he has a plan for each one of us.

Dear Father,

Your will drives our lives. Please help us to remember to ask for your counsel as we plan and evaluate our careers. Give us the courage we need to boldly seek your will. Amen.

Recipe for Service

Over the years, I have discovered a recipe for maintaining a positive service attitude. It is not a secret recipe handed down from generation to generation; the ingredients are well known, but we tend to forget them from time to time. A positive service attitude is difficult to maintain because numerous forces can work against it. Rude people, long hours, impossible demands, and uncaring bosses can beat the service attitude right out of even the most stouthearted educator! With the right recipe, we can keep our attitudes fully prepared!

The ingredients of a positive service attitude are as follows:

1. Humility

We are to be humble as we lead and serve others. Our thoughts and actions are selfless in nature, and we do not let our egos become inflated.

2. Golden Rule

We always treat others in the same way we wish to be treated. We are kind, caring, forgiving, patient, and empathetic toward everyone.

3. Call to Serve

We have an intense desire to help others and make a positive difference in their lives. We are focused on meeting other people's needs and creating the best possible future for our students.

4. Perseverance

We are thick-skinned and able to handle rejection, scorn, and harsh attitudes. Not everyone will appreciate our efforts to serve; however, we will never give up.

This can be a difficult recipe to mix and store, so Paul gave us some good advice:

> Never be lazy in your work, but serve the Lord enthusiastically.
>
> Romans 12:11

As servant leaders, we have energy and enthusiasm unmatched by other leaders because God is the additional ingredient in our recipe that is the never-fail ingredient for success. God supports us and strengthens us to meet any challenge we might face. With faith in God as our main ingredient for success, how can we not be filled with endless energy and enthusiasm?

Dear Father,

It is not easy to be service-minded all of the time; but with your guidance, we can do it. Grant us the patience, perseverance, and enthusiasm that we need to serve your children well. Amen.

Matt Stephen, Ed.D.

February

February is a month for celebrating relationships. Valentine's Day helps us to focus on our mates. We also celebrate our relationships with children and other adults in our lives. As we focus on our loved ones, we are providing a role model of humility and selflessness for our children. They need to witness a true service attitude–thinking of others first and a willingness to sacrifice self for others.

The pace seems to slow down in February. It is cold outside. Often the weather is too miserable for us to go anywhere, so "Cabin Fever" can begin to set in. We are looking into the future toward Spring Break, and we realize that it is still six weeks away. We can help accelerate the slow pace of February through celebrations such as National Freedom Day, National School Counseling Week, Brotherhood/Sisterhood Week and Presidents' Day.

Standardized and End-of-Year assessments are looming over our students and us. We realize that our time to prepare is getting shorter. Accountability is important, but it seems to overshadow our real purpose of creating the best future for our children. Working together as a team, we can overcome the challenges of standardized testing and accountability.

We can remember our New Year's Resolutions. God's fruits of the spirit are there for us if we are living in him. We can do all within our power to shelter his children from the harmfulness of this world. We can remember to ask for God's help as we lead his children. It is too awesome of a responsibility to attempt on our own!

The Three C's

As a servant leader, I try my best to always maintain the three C's (cool, calm, and collected). I hate it when someone successfully pushes my emotional buttons and I lose control of a situation. I lose my cool composure, and I sink to my adversary's level of resolving conflicts. I immediately feel guilty and ashamed because I let someone else control my behavior. I know that I tend to lose my self-control when my defenses are down. It happens more often when I am tired, stressed, busy, under pressure, worried, upset, or not feeling well.

Leaders are expected to exhibit the three C's at all times even when others are in a panic. Unfortunately, there is no magic pill or mantra for remaining calm in a storm. Ineffective leaders lose the three C's quickly when under pressure while good leaders persevere and hope for the best.

Paul tells servant leaders how God wants us to behave:

For God is not a God of disorder but of peace.

1 Corinthians 14:33

Christian servant leaders have an advantage over other leaders when it comes to crisis moments. They have the gift of God's peace that sustains them through anything. God's peace transcends earthly problems. Peace here on earth is fragile because it depends upon the human interactions. God's peace is unshakable, unchanging and eternal because God is the bedrock to this peace. Even as servant leaders, we are still human and our faith in God's help can be shaken when we are in crisis. To remain cool, calm and collected, we can persevere and maintain our faith that God never leaves us—especially in times of crisis.

We can pray for God's peace; so that as his leaders, we can be reflective, serene, in control, proactive, encouraging to others, unshakable, and courageous. God will ensure that we can maintain the three C's.

Dear Father,

Thank you for your peace. It will keep me cool, calm, and collected as I face all challenges. Your peace is my peace when I am working with you. Amen.

Matt Stephen, Ed.D.

Take Time to Play

Educators are serious people. We are called to our profession by the highest authority, so we are totally devoted to our teaching. We give ourselves totally to our work because our children's lives are affected by everything that we do and say, and we know that the quality of our work affects our children's future. Each day we get up early to plan our day, arrive at school and work all day, stay late to work some more, and then take work home with us. We often sacrifice weekends, weeknights, family activities, and sometimes even church activities in order to keep up with our schoolwork. To add to our self-inflicted pressure the federal government, our state legislators, our communities, our school boards, and students' parents expect results and expect it now!

God gives us the answer to daily pressures through one of King David's songs:

> Give your burdens to the Lord, and he will take care of you. He will not permit the godly to slip and fall.
>
> Psalm 55:22

We are permitted to cast our troubles to the Lord and allow him to carry them for us! We are also assured that he will not allow us to slip or fall. Think of this image. We can hoist a hundred-pound suitcase full of worries and burdens to God, and he will carry it for us. This frees us to walk light-footed and carefree. Not only will God carry these burdens for us, he is right beside us to ensure that we do not slip and fall! If we can allow ourselves to do this each day, there will be considerably more room in our attitudes for positive thoughts and service spirit.

To further relieve the pressure, we can take time to play. We all play in our own way: sports, hobbies, reading, shopping, socializing, and music to name just a few. Taking time to play can help us put things into perspective. Play can help us realize that there is a completely different side of ourselves that we too often ignore. Playing, in whatever form we choose, is fun!

Our children will remind us to play. I received a wake-up call one day when my daughter asked me if I was in a good mood. I told her that I was and asked her why she asked me that question. She replied, "Because you are laughing and joking with us!" I realized then that I had been taking life too seriously. If it had become an unusual event for my children to see me laugh and play, then something needed to change!

We can play each day on the job by laughing. There are many reasons why we should laugh. Laughter is music to the soul. Many people believe that laughter has a healing power. Laughter is free, and it can be shared. Laughter can be planned or it can be spontaneous. Most of all, laughter can help relieve the pressures in our jobs. Laugh when you pat a child on the head and the nurse looks at you funny because she is checking him for head lice. Laugh when a child gives you five after wiping his nose. Laugh when the bus arrives 30 minutes late to school. Laugh because laughter, like play, helps us keep things in perspective.

Matt Stephen, Ed.D.

We as Christians have the ultimate reason to be happy regardless of what the world hands us. As Jesus said:

> Be happy about it! Be very glad! For a great reward awaits you in heaven.
>
> Matthew 5:12

Once in heaven, we will wonder why we worried so much about trivial things here on earth. Perhaps we should worry less and take advantage of what fun and laughter has to offer us each day.

Dear Father,

Thank you for the gift of happiness. Please help us to focus on our earthly mission to joyfully serve others. At the same time, help us to focus on the eternal reward that you have given to us. Amen.

Judging and Changing People

Everyone has something in his or her life that needs to be improved. In fact, many people have irritating habits or an aspect of their character that people around them would like to see improved. Other people have the answers to all of their problems if they would just ask! However, changing people is not easy, and sometimes impossible. Believe it or not, some people do not want to change their ways just to please others!

At school, we sometimes do not work well together because of our differences. If we are willing to tolerate these differences among one another, this can lead to a better understanding of others. This understanding can lead to a better acceptance of others. Once a foundation of acceptance is laid, we can move toward celebrating our differences. Once we are able to celebrate, we can then work together and draw upon one another's strengths. We count upon one another's strengths to complement our own talents and help minimize our weaknesses. This pooling of strengths is what makes our schools great!

Jesus gives us good advice about judging and changing others:

> Stop judging others, and you will not be judged. For others will treat you as you treat them. Whatever measure you use in judging others, it will be used to measure how you are judged. And why worry about a speck in your friend's eye when you have a log in your own? Hypocrite! First get rid of the log

from your own eye; then perhaps you will see well enough to deal with the speck in your friend's eye.

Matthew 7:1–3, 5

It is hard for us to see our own teeny-tiny flaws while the huge imperfections of others seem to jump out at us. Jesus tells us not to work on other people's flaws until we are rid of our own. For most of us, getting rid of all personal flaws could take some serious time and effort! Jesus wants us to help our brothers, but in a spirit of love, not revenge. We tend to point out other people's flaws out of spite or jealousy rather than in a spirit of helping them to improve.

Think of someone that you really do not like. Now ask yourself why you do not like this person. What quality does this person possess that causes you not to like him? Now examine that quality and turn it around. What is good about this quality? Reflect on this until you derive an answer. Now you will see the good that this person can bring to a relationship. For example, someone who is overbearing or pushy can bring a quality of assertiveness to the group. With a little bit of work, this person can be an asset to the team rather than a liability.

The bottom line is that when changes need to be made, we cannot force others to change. We only have control over what we do and how we react to what others do. If we can change our perceptions, attitudes, or actions then maybe those changes will affect others around us. We cannot control the behavior of others, but we can be there to provide a positive role model for those who want to change their behavior.

Dear Father,

We are far from perfect. We will clean up our own lives before we start in on improving those around us. Help us to be there when others need us. Give us the wisdom to help those who ask for our assistance. Amen.

Last Place

One of the most difficult tasks for people to accomplish is to ignore themselves and tend to others' needs. This is a foreign concept for many in today's society. We are in the habit of seeking out what pleasures us. The media entices us to indulge ourselves and pursue our every desire. We are encouraged to seek pleasure now and pay later. We are taught by society that we should look out for ourselves first and strive to be number one. We are encouraged to win at all costs. This type of lifestyle calls for selfishness. We must constantly search out what is best for us. If our hearts and minds are full of ourselves and our own wants, there is not enough room for God and his will. We are told throughout the Bible that we must leave ourselves and enter the lives of others. Only then are we free to allow Jesus fully into our lives. Only then can we be number one to the one who truly matters.

Jesus tells us what we must do:

> Then he called his disciples and the crowds to come over and listen. "If any of you wants to be my follower," he told them, "you must put aside your selfish ambition, shoulder your cross, and follow me."
>
> Mark 8:34

Jesus tells us to put aside our self-ambitions and pleasures. We are to minimize interest in ourselves and turn our interest towards others. This is all our children are asking of us. They simply want us to take an interest in their lives. They do not care about the long hours of planning, accuracy of the assessments, validity of new curriculum, or the success of instructional methods. They simply want to know that they are important to us.

Jesus is the ultimate servant leader. He modeled servant leadership for us and told us how to lead his children. Putting aside our self-ambitions and pleasures is no easy task for the average human being; therefore, we must strive to be superhuman in order to lead God's children. When it comes to making decisions in our lives, God has set our priorities as follows: consider God first, then all others, then ourselves. Notice that we come in a distant third. We are in last place! Although we place ourselves last, God places us first now; and he will place us first as we enter our eternal reward.

Dear Father,

Please help us to leave ourselves and enter the lives of others. Only then can we truly serve your children. Although we are to consider ourselves last, we know that you consider us first. Amen.

Matt Stephen, Ed.D.

Indecision

As educators, we make hundreds of decisions each day. Most decisions are easy to make because ample information is available and the consequences are not great. Sometimes we are faced with big decisions that greatly affect our present and future lives. When faced with these types of decisions, what do we do? To whom do we turn?

God speaks to us a great deal in silence. He doesn't write on our walls, marker boards, or computer screens. We have to be still to hear his voice. Many times, he speaks to us through our "gut." We hear him through our emotions and inner feelings. This voice or feeling is called by many names: the Holy Spirit, guardian angel, our conscience, gut feeling, or that small, inner voice. Regardless of what we call it, this voice is God speaking to us!

I can attest that I feel different when I am walking the wrong path. I know when I have made a bad decision, have a negative attitude, or have treated others wrong because I get an uncomfortable feeling inside of me. Once I make the right decision and remedy the situation, I feel better. I know this was God making me uncomfortable.

How does God speak to us? How does he show us the way and help us make the right decisions? Here are some ways for us to hear God:

1. Pray about the decision. Give God an opportunity to speak to us.

2. Listen to our inner feelings.

3. Listen to others. God sometimes speaks to us through the most unexpected people or events.

4. Take action. God will let us know if we are on the right path.

Advice was given to us a long time ago about thinking and praying too much or too long without taking action. At the edge of the Red Sea, Moses was praying to God about what to do as the Egyptians were in hot pursuit:

> Then the Lord said to Moses, "Why are you crying out to me? Tell the people to get moving!"
>
> Exodus 14: 15

God wants us to slow down and pray to ask for his advice and help, but there are also times when he wants us to get moving. This is hard to do when we are afraid. However, King David showed his confidence that the Lord will take care of us:

> Though I am surrounded by troubles, you will preserve me against the anger of my enemies. You will clench your fist against my angry enemies! Your power will save me. The Lord will work out his plans for my life.
>
> Psalm 138:7–8

It is nice to know that we have the perfect backup when we need help with our decisions. We can always move forward in confidence that God is on our side and that his power is with us. If we maintain faith in God and keep moving toward his will, he will block the wrong paths and open up the right ones!

Dear Father,

Help us to slow down and hear your words. Then give us the courage to take action for your children's sake. Amen.

Freedom Bound

As educators, we go to great effort to instill patriotism and an appreciation for freedom in our children. We teach about how our forefathers battled tyranny to create a new nation. We explore the history of our country by studying the lives of Americans who sought freedom as well as the events where our ancestors fought for freedom. Our quest for freedom can be explored through historical documents, art, literature, and music.

"My Country, Tis of Thee" is a patriotic song with a great message. It basically says that our country was founded upon our fathers' faith in God and his plan for our freedom. The song also asks for God's guidance and protection for our nation. We are truly fortunate to live in a nation that believes in freedom and equality for all people. Although our society has its flaws, most of us make a special effort to respect one another's rights and live peacefully with one another.

However, it seems that we are moving away from the ideal of grounding our society upon God's will. Human selfishness has led us to move away from God's laws and move toward selfish pursuits for individual freedom. Consequently, the farther we move away from God's laws, the less free we become as a society. Without God's laws, we must worry about violence, poverty, war, prejudice, greed, anger, infidelity, and revenge. These worries bind us in fear for self-preservation and prevent us from thinking of others.

Paul warns us about getting too involved in the ways of the world:

Matt Stephen, Ed.D.

And as Christ's soldier, do not let yourself become tied up in the affairs of this life, for then you cannot satisfy the one who enlisted you in his army.

2 Timothy 2:4

To be truly free, we must free ourselves from earthly matters so we can concentrate on pleasing God. With God's peace in our hearts and minds, we can free ourselves of worrying strictly about ourselves and turn our attention to the needs of others. We can best serve our nation by teaching our children to return to God's will. Freedom through God's laws was the original intent of our forefathers, and this is the freedom upon which our children can rely for the future of our nation.

Dear Father,

Help us as a nation to realize that only through your laws can we truly be free. Thank you for your peace and the freedom that peace gives us to serve others. Amen.

Thank You for Trouble

Can life be trouble-free? Perhaps we can create an illusion of a trouble-free existence by ignoring problems that arise, but ignoring these problems does not make them go away. As servant leaders, we cannot run away from problems because we are troubleshooters. Problems and conflicts arise daily, and they are taken to the leader to be solved. We can grow and develop our servant leadership through dealing with troublesome experiences. I estimate that students, parents, colleagues, and administrators bring dozens of problems daily to teachers to be solved. It is quite unfair, but we mostly deal with problems that we did not even have the luxury of starting!

God tells us that fiery trials test our faith and help to burn off our imperfections:

> These trials are only to test your faith, to show that it is strong and pure. It is being tested as fire tests and purifies gold - and your faith is far more precious to God that mere gold. So if your faith remains strong after being tried by fiery trials, it will bring you much praise and glory and honor on the day when Jesus Christ is revealed to the whole world.
>
> 1 Peter 1:7

Dealing with trouble can make us stronger and wiser. Troublesome situations come at school administrators, teachers, and staff from all different directions: students, parents, district leadership, state and federal school agencies, media, and special interest groups. One might

Matt Stephen, Ed.D.

believe that I have left my good senses, but I believe when we see trouble coming, we should say, "Thank you, God, for the trouble that is coming. I know that this experience will help me grow to be a stronger leader." As crazy as this might sound, this attitude helps us look forward to all situations, both positive and negative. Do not mistake me for one who enjoys conflict. I do not look for trouble. But when I see it coming, I might as well thank God for the lesson that I am about to learn!

God tells us that a successful servant leader should be strong in character and ready for anything. To do this, we must strengthen our faith by enduring the trials that the world has to offer. Our payoff for building and maintaining a strong faith will be honor and glory from God!

Dear Father,

Thank you for the trials and tests that I face daily. I know that it makes me stronger, wiser, and more able to serve you. I will stay close to you and rely upon your guidance throughout the day, especially when trouble comes looking for me. Amen.

Team-Building

In professional sports, everyone has their favorite teams. Fans talk about their favorite teams constantly and pack the stadiums to see them play. Devoted fans know how their teams are faring and support them 100 percent. They anticipate opportunities to see their teams play. They celebrate their wins and despair in their defeats. Fans also have their favorite players whom they admire. They talk about their favorite players and buy clothes and memorabilia that remind them of their heroes.

As participants in amateur sports, we can experience these emotions for ourselves as we play together as teammates. We support one another, celebrate our victories, and console one another in our defeats. We form bonds with one another that are unique and powerful.

I wish education teams were more like sports teams. A big difference between education and sports teams involves the concept of winning and losing. Sports teams receive immediate feedback as to a win or a loss, and they receive immediate data as to who contributed to that win or loss. As educators, we often do not know if we are winning or losing. Winning and losing is either not clearly defined or the definitions fluctuate greatly from state to state or district to district. We do not know for certain if our game plans are working, so we are changing them constantly—often before they have a chance to succeed or fail. We aren't sure who our superstar teachers are, and we can't seem to get our fans to pack our schools!

We, as professional educators, can learn much in the area of team building from the sports profession. We can

Matt Stephen, Ed.D.

envision a common goal and pursue it with a passion. We can encourage one another to do our best. We can celebrate our victories and take our defeats personally. We can show support by giving one another high fives when things are going well and encouraging one another in our setbacks.

As in our physical development, we move through several stages as we grow in our professional lives. We begin our careers in the dependent stage. As new teachers, we depend on someone to train us in our first few years. We move to independence as we see that we can make it on our own. In this stage, we can work alone in confidence that we can do as well or better than those around us can. Unfortunately, this can lead to an isolationism where each teacher is an "island" and believes he or she needs help from no one. After the independence stage is achieved, it is crucial that we move to the interdependence stage. At this stage, we pool our strengths and work together to create a product better than one could produce alone. Only as a team can we give our children the best possible educational experience. It takes an entire school staff to create a great learning environment!

Paul tells us how to treat others on our teams:

> Don't be selfish; don't live to make a good impression on others. Be humble, thinking of others as better than yourself. Don't think only about you own affairs, but be interested in others, too, and what they are doing.
>
> Philippians 2:3–4

As staff members, if we act through selfish ambition or conceit, we become our own worst enemies. Looking out for the interests of others means making decisions based upon what is best for the entire school, even if our own best interests are not served. A team concept also means supporting one another and holding other people's needs above our own desires. It also means watching our colleagues' backs and picking one another up when we are down. Let's find the team spirit in ourselves and get excited about winning. Let's celebrate our successes and enjoy each step we take every day!

Dear Father,

It takes all of us to raise your children according to your will. Help us to put others first and consider ourselves last. Guide us to support one another in our efforts to best serve your children. Amen.

Forgiveness

Have you witnessed the awesome power of forgiveness? I have seen and experienced it many times myself. I have seen it change the lives of educators, students, and parents. A person's life can be overwhelmed by the need to forgive or be forgiven. We find that once forgiveness takes place, life is totally different. Everything looks, smells, sounds, and feels better. Life seems to have more meaning, and one can actually feel several pounds lighter!

If a person is currently in a situation where forgiveness is needed, it is easy enough to correct. One might be on either side of the issue. If one needs to forgive, one can drop one's pride and do it. If one needs forgiveness, one can drop one's pride and ask for it. If the other person is unwilling to forgive, one can talk to God and ask for his assistance. God's wisdom and guidance easily supersedes our human faults.

God has advice for us on forgiveness:

> You must make allowance for each other's faults and forgive the person who offends you. Remember, the Lord forgave you, so you must forgive others.
>
> Colossians 3:13

An important point to remember is that God will not forgive us if we do not forgive others (Matthew 6:14). This is a very scary concept! We cannot expect something from God that we are unwilling to give ourselves. We must be willing to forgive. Yes, we can live out our lives without forgiving others. We can put these people out of our minds, move forward with our lives, and never give them another thought; however, one day we will face God's judgment for not forgiving them. Forgiving is not something we do for others. Forgiving is something we do for ourselves!

Think of your school's climate. Is there an overall air of forgiveness? Do people hold grudges, or are they willing to forgive and forget? If not, get together, discuss the power of freedom through forgiveness, and push for it at your school. Forgiveness is an important quality for the adults to model in our schools. Our children must learn to forgive one another, and they will learn best by watching us forgive one another.

Dear Father,

Forgive us where we have failed you and help us to forgive our neighbors. We need the freedom, peace and happiness that forgiveness can bring. Help us to establish a forgiving atmosphere at our school. Amen.

Matt Stephen, Ed.D.

The Wrong Crowd

Have you ever told a parent that his or her child had fallen in with the wrong crowd? I have said these words on many occasions when good children begin to follow the wrong lead. It is imperative to redirect these children before something goes very wrong. We, as educators, know what terrific influence peer pressure has on children. A child with good discipline and moral guidance can fall into the trap of listening to their peers over their parents. It amazes me to see the terrible things some good children will do or say to please their peers. We have all witnessed sad and embarrassing situations which involved students bowing to peer pressure.

What about adults? Are we also influenced by our peers? Are we susceptible to influence from the wrong people? It is a fact that we become like those with whom we associate. I have seen some educators begin their careers with very positive attitudes; yet in a few short years, they are as negative as those whom they chose to be their professional mentors.

Often, we listen to others' experiences and ideas as we formulate our attitudes toward education. We sometimes accept other people's perceptions as truths and weave them into our own thoughts. We then act upon these attitudes and beliefs and perpetuate them. We help to spread others' attitudes and beliefs as they become our own. We can ask ourselves if the ideas that we are helping to spread are constructive or destructive, and we can take a close look at the people with whom we associate at school. Are they groundbreaking, risk-taking, education supporting, customer pleasing, positive minded child advocates?

Paul tells us not to be wrapped up in the ways of this world:

> Don't copy the behaviors and customs of this world, but let God transform you into a new person by changing the way you think. Then you will know what God wants you to do, and you will know how good and pleasing and perfect his will really is.
>
> Romans 12:2

What great advice this is! We are not supposed to blindly accept and follow the ways of this world. We are to think for ourselves, consult with God, and make a conscious effort to be new, fresh, and different. Once we do this, we will know what God wants us to do - no more guessing. The reward is that we will learn to see through our own experiences how good life can really be.

Dear Father,

Thank you for making us individual thinkers. We will look for other positive thinkers with whom to associate at work and in our personal lives. Please help us to stay positive and supportive of your children. Amen.

Matt Stephen, Ed.D.

March

March is the month of the long stretch to Spring Break. Everyone is exhausted and this seems to affect everything we say and do. Patience and forgiveness are especially important at this time of year. We can focus on the importance of tolerance and flexibility when dealing with others this month. Our students need to see us model these guiding principles. It is important to keep the proper focus of serving God and others.

The beginning of March usually offers Public Schools Week and Open House. These activities alone are enough to keep us busy. As tired as we are, we need to celebrate our profession because we are the foundation of our society. Collectively, we help shape the future of our country! Toward the end of the month, we celebrate Spring Break. This vacation rejuvenates us and gives us desperately needed energy to survive the next two months. During this vacation week, we are allowed to focus on ourselves. We can spend the week relaxing or playing hard. We get to decide what is best for us.

Usually, winter begins to release its icy hold on us during the month of March. The first day of spring falls within this month, and the spring-like weather beckons us to partake in some outside activities. This is a good time to praise our Lord for his beautiful world and the newness of life that spring represents. We can also rejoice in springtime because our students can get outside each day to burn off some of their energy!

Matt Stephen, Ed.D.

Gentleness

Some people are amazed that children can approach a principal these days with a smile and a hug. They ask, "What happened to the days when students were afraid of the principal?" They further state, "It used to be that when you saw the principal, you knew you were in big trouble." Principals once carried big paddles and spoke with loud voices. Leadership by intimidation is on its way out, and it certainly has not been my choice of leadership style. I like to speak softly, put my trust in others, and use the "big stick" only when necessary. In other words, I prefer to be a gentle leader.

As educators, we are charged with keeping our emotions under control even as those around us are losing their cool. It is very difficult to remain calm while there are storms all around. We may appear to lose a confrontation when we restrain our emotions and maintain control. Some people believe that aggressive behavior and foul language will help them prevail. However, we know that conflicts are best settled by maintaining a level head and calm demeanor.

Some people see gentleness as a sign of weakness. However, as educators, we know that it can take great strength to restrain our emotions and remain gentle. We are stronger than those who lose their self-control and lash out at others.

God tells us from where our true strength will come:

> The Sovereign Lord, The Holy One of Israel, says, "Only in returning to me and waiting for

me will you be saved. In quietness and confidence
is your strength."

Isaiah 30:15

God tells us that our strength lies in our quiet confidence in
him. God can give us the strength we need to remain calm.
He can give us the "thick skin" we need in order to stay in
control. We can remain confident that God will be our "big
stick," and that he will give us the strength that we need to
prevail. We often find ourselves in the middle of conflict. We
certainly do not look for trouble, but it can easily find us. Paul
gives us directions to follow as troubles approach us:

> Again I say, don't get involved in foolish, ignorant
> arguments that only start fights. The Lord's ser-
> vants must not quarrel but must be kind to every-
> one. They must be able to teach effectively and be
> patient with difficult people.

2 Timothy 2:23–25

We are told to avoid conflict. As a servant of the Lord,
we are instructed to go out of our way to see that peace
and harmony are maintained. This is not easy. It is often
difficult to restrain ourselves from saying what is on our
minds (some of us have sore tongues from the constant
biting). It is also made clear to us that God expects us to
be humble, patient, and gentle toward his children. It is
reassuring to know that God is aware of how difficult it is
for us to stay calm amidst attacks. He is prepared to offer
us the strength we need to overcome our own emotions.

Dear Father,

Please help us to be gentle toward others. In times of confrontation, keep us calm so that we can do your will. Help us to be patient with your children so that we can teach them to be patient and gentle with one another. Amen.

Professional Dress Code

The professional dress codes at schools often seem to get more attention than they really deserve. We measure skirts; carefully define clothing items such as shorts, skorts, and jeans; assign acceptable degrees of tightness to clothing; and clearly define acceptable wear for spirit days, casual days and normal workdays. I have always been a fan of allowing the staff to create their own professional dress code. I found that once the dress code was created and published in the staff handbook, much time and effort was then needed to enforce the code. Personally, I was always too intimidated to measure skirts or examine necklines and tightness of clothes. When it came to female dress code infractions, coward that I am, I left that to my female assistant principals. However, please know that I was more than willing to handle the male infractions.

I am not sure if certain clothing stimulates teachers and students to perform better, so I will leave that debate to my learned colleagues. However, I am sure of one thing–God gives us a dress code which is critical to our success.

Peter tells us which part of a dress code is most important:

> Don't be concerned about the outward beauty that depends on fancy hairstyles, expensive jewelry, or beautiful clothes. You should be known for the beauty that comes from within, the unfading beauty of a gentle and quiet spirit, which is so precious to God.
>
> 1 Peter 3:3–4

Matt Stephen, Ed.D.

Imagine the wonderful climates that would exist in our schools if everyone adhered to God's dress code. If everyone wore gentle and quiet spirits, we would no longer need security police, discipline codes or alternative schools. Paul tells us that our dress code must always be changing for the better:

> There must be a spiritual renewal of your thoughts and attitudes. You must display a new nature because you are a new person, created in God's likeness—righteous, holy, and true.
> Ephesians 4:23–24

We should never be satisfied that we have completely complied with God's dress code. We should always be searching ourselves for better attitudes and more godly behavior.

Dear Father,

Thank you for assigning us the ultimate dress code. Each day we will wear our gentle, quiet spirits for your children. Amen.

When to Let Go

When I was younger, I thought I could solve any problem that crossed my path. Experience has taught me that this is not true. There are some situations that I cannot solve. There are children whom I cannot get to conform. There are parents with whom I cannot negotiate. There are staff members whose attitudes toward children and education I cannot make more positive. There are bosses whom I cannot get to listen to me.

I do not like it when a situation seems to be out of my control or influence. I do not like it when a problem cannot be solved at my level. I do not like to admit that I failed to accomplish something on my own. It takes a lot of courage for me to ask for help because it requires me to admit that I cannot do it alone.

In spite of my distaste for failure, I have learned that I cannot save every child on my own. Some situations are beyond my expertise. I owe it to my students to let go of my ego and seek help from others when I need it. I know that help is available from parents, colleagues, professionals outside of public education, community members, religious leaders, and God himself.

We often forget to go to God with our problems. We exhaust all of our own efforts first. Then when things are really "messed-up," we finally turn to him with our problems. We are told that once we go to God for his help, we accomplish our tasks with ease and even go beyond our original expectations:

Matt Stephen, Ed. D.

Now glory be to God! By his mighty power at work within us, he is able to accomplish infinitely more that we would ever dare to ask or hope.

Ephesians 3:20

The infinite power to teach all children and to solve all problems lies within each of us. All we have to do is let go of our desire to work alone and ask God to work through us.

Dear Father,

We know that we cannot do everything by ourselves. Please remind us to call upon you for help each day. Only with your guidance and assistance can we make the best positive difference in your children's lives. Amen.

Humor

Singing with joy is easy to do during Sunday worship service, but how do we come to God singing with joy during the workweek? We do it through laughter! We can express our joy of life and appreciation for God's peace daily through our laughter. I have often heard that laughter is music to the soul. How many times has a good laugh made us feel good or helped us forget our troubles even for just a few minutes? There are scientific studies that claim that laughter can lower one's blood pressure and boost one's immune system. I suspect that laughter may one day be proven to reverse the aging process or burn calories at an astronomical rate!

Laughter is a sign that we are not taking things too seriously and that we are at peace with the world and ourselves. If we can see the humor in everyday trials, they cannot overpower us. Laughter can free us from focusing on the small problems in our lives. Most of these little problems will not have a long-range effect on our lives, so we should not give them more power than they deserve. If the small problems are stacking up and we find it difficult to laugh, we should seek out a person or situation that we know will tickle our funny bone. A good laugh will help us to regain our proper focus.

Humor is all around us in this world. We can locate our sense of humor and find joy daily in our jobs. I never run out of funny stories about kids whom I have had the privilege to serve! Here are some gems from my world:

Matt Stephen, Ed.D.

- Once I said to a kindergartner who was about to perform the Pledge of Allegiance for the morning announcements, "Are you ready to do the pledge?" He replied, "Sure, I practiced last night in the bathtub!"

- One Friday afternoon while waiting for the school bus, I said to a student, "Tomorrow is Saturday. You can sleep in." Her reply was, "But Mr. Stephen, I always sleep inside the house!"

- One day, I was scolding a first grade student for not paying attention to his teacher. He suddenly looked down at his stomach and said, "Oh no! Now my bellybutton is bothering me!"

- A story written and illustrated by a first grade student: "My dog died. A tree fell on him. He wasn't looking where he was going."

Jesus tells us that we may have peace through him:

> I have told you all this so that you may have peace in me. Here on earth you will have many trials and sorrows. But take heart, because I have overcome the world.
>
> John 16:33

Laughter will give us peace and joy in this crazy world. It will be easier to experience God's peace and joy if we focus on the wonderful fact that Jesus has overcome the world, and he is greater than any earthly trials or sorrows.

Dear Father,

We want to keep laughing. Please help us to stay focused on your will for our lives. Help us to focus on the joys of life rather than the little troubles that sometimes seem to stack up. We want to experience joy and peace as we serve you and your children. Amen.

Can We Take It?

"How much of this can I take?" How many times have we asked ourselves this question lately? My guess is more often than we would have liked. Thinking of all the children with poor self-discipline, the hours of grading papers, the after-school meetings, and the weekends spent planning lessons is enough to make anyone consider throwing in the towel. People all around us (supervisors, colleagues, students, parents, community, media, and school boards) have very high expectations of us, and they can be quite abusive. With all of the long hours, hard work, thanklessness, pressures, and criticisms surrounding us, it is easy to wonder, "How much can I take before I give up on this job?"

We know that we should not grow weary or lose heart because in the long run we will reap benefits for doing good things here on earth. This is sound but difficult advice because we like to receive immediate rewards for what we do. Often, our immediate pressures and troubles do not quickly melt away simply because we are trying to concentrate on eternal rewards. It will take more than hot baths to make some of our headaches go away. We can reflect and take a hard look at ourselves and our students and ask, "Is my presence here enriching these students' lives?" Once we have honestly answered this question, we are ready to examine our options. If we choose to stay in education, we will want to seek the endurance that we will need to keep serving God's children and to maintain a positive state of mind.

We can discover the endurance that we need if we keep up our courage and maintain our joy and trust in the Lord:

But Christ, the faithful Son, was in charge of the entire household. And we are God's household, if we keep up our courage and remain confident in our hope in Christ.

Hebrews 3:6

Our reward for trusting God is joy. Happiness and joy are not the same emotion. Circumstances around us need to be positive in order for us to be happy. Joy, on the other hand, is not dependent upon our circumstances here on earth. Joy is the firm foundation laid through faith in God and in his plan for our lives. Joy is the security of knowing that God is with us every minute of every day. Joy is knowing that we are unconditionally loved and celebrated by God throughout our earthly and everlasting lives. With rewards like these, we should be able to endure our trials and tribulations one hundred fold! We can remind one another of the joy and strength that God has to offer us. Let's remember to do this daily!

Dear Father,

Please energize us when we become weary as we try to accomplish your will. Please renew us by rekindling our joy of serving others. We will trust you to give us the endurance we need to face our daily challenges. Amen.

Matt Stephen, Ed.D.

How Great Art Thou?

Have you ever asked yourself, "How good am I?" In today's competitive world, this is a very valid question. As we struggle to do our best, it is only natural to want to compare ourselves to others. Many of us compete with one another as we climb the corporate ladder or look for the success that will elevate us above the rest. We are often competitive as we work together. We like to see our students create the best projects, perform the best on standardized tests, and exhibit the best behavior throughout the school. Some of us like to compete for educator awards and receive recognition for our accomplishments. We tend to equate our job success with our self-worth. We can be great servant leaders; but when we begin to congratulate ourselves for our successful accomplishments, we begin to fail.

Success can be one of the greatest dangers we face in life. Praise from our fellow man can also be dangerous. It can lead us to think too much of ourselves. Success here on earth can separate us from God. As we trust more in our jobs, our families, our homes, our material possessions, and ourselves, we trust less in God. The more we focus on our own achievements and ourselves, the less we think of God and his purpose for our lives.

God searches our hearts for our true motives:

> I, the Lord, search all hearts and examine secret motives. I give all people their due rewards, according to what their actions deserve.
>
> Jeremiah 17:10

We should examine what it is that drives us. Is it a desire to be admired by others, or is it to give our best to God's children so that they will prosper? God knows, and he is preparing our reward in accordance to our motives and our deeds!

Dear Father,

Thank you for giving us the desire to be the best. Help us balance our desire to be the best with our desire to do our best for your children. Amen.

Matt Stephen, Ed.D.

One Good Friday

One Good Friday
many years ago,
our world as we know it
hit its lowest of low.

We showed our most human traits
fear, jealousy, greed and deceit,
as we took God's greatest gift
and trampled him under our feet.

Because we did not understand
we demanded death in God's name.
So Jesus walked to his crucifixion
thus adding to our shame.

The world spent the next day and darkest night
with no more hope for future light.

The third day, God again proved his love
with one more miracle for us to see.
He collected up all of our ugly sins
and set each one of us free.

The one we murdered was not man alone,
his victory—an open grave.
For he is Jesus, Son of God, King of Kings,
his mission—our lives to save.

Today his resurrection gives us hope,
prayers to pray and songs to sing.
Because of Jesus' sacrifice and God's grace
we now have life everlasting.

Jesus sums it all up for us in one sentence:

> For God so loved the world that he gave his only
> Son, so that everyone who believes in him will not
> perish but have eternal life.
>
> John 3:16

Dear Father,

Thank you for the gift of eternal life through your Son's
supreme sacrifice. Help us to slow down and meditate on
your love and grace during this holy week. Amen.

Matt Stephen, Ed.D.

Setting Priorities

What guides our thoughts, words and actions? What guides our setting of priorities? Do we set our goals according to personal wants and desires, or do we consult God's will for direction? We generate short-term and long-term goals for all aspects of our lives. We may not be fully aware of these goals because we have not verbalized them aloud or in writing. Leaders should take the time to write down their short and long-term goals. We can fill in the short and long-term goals for our personal and professional lives, but God has filled in the blanks for us regarding our spiritual lives. Here is a template for writing short and long-term goals:

	Short-Term Goals	Long-Term Goals
Personal Life		
Professional Life		
Spiritual Life	• Love God with all my heart, soul, and mind • Love my neighbor as I love myself • Daily communication with God • Live life every day according to God's will	• Eternal Life with God in Heaven

	• Experience God's wisdom and peace in our lives here on Earth • Lead others to God	

Religious leaders were always trying to outsmart Jesus by getting him to speak against God. One leader thought he cornered Jesus when he asked him which of the Ten Commandments was the greatest. Jesus turned the tables on him by rolling all Ten Commandments into the "greatest commandment" to love God with all our heart, soul, and mind and to love our neighbors as ourselves. As servant leaders, we cannot ask God, "Which of your rules are the most important for us to follow?" We cannot cut corners by following only some of God's rules because all of his rules are essential to our success as servant leaders.

Jesus also tells us that we are in trouble if we turn away from him:

> But Jesus told him, "Anyone who puts a hand to the plow and then looks back is not fit for the Kingdom of God."
>
> Luke 9:62

Our personal and professional goals are important, but we should be aware that they can cause us to be distracted from our ultimate goal of eternal life. Our personal and

Matt Stephen, Ed.D.

professional goals should complement our spiritual goals–
not conflict with them. We are not fit for God's kingdom if
we let ourselves be distracted by earthly goals and pleasures.

Dear Father,

Help us to keep our relationships with you as top
priority. We will not be distracted by earthly goals and
pleasures. Amen.

Truth or Dare

"Truth or Dare" is a game where a person either tells the truth to the group or accepts a dare to accomplish in place of the truth. Often, one finds that telling the truth or taking the dare can be equally embarrassing. In other words, one has to decide to what degree it is important to either tell or avoid telling the truth.

We play Truth or Dare all the time. We sometimes avoid telling the truth to parents because we think that they are not prepared to hear the blunt truth about their children's academic or behavioral progress. We sometimes hold our honest feedback with our students in order to maintain their self-esteem. We are sometimes dishonest with colleagues in order to spare feelings and preserve relationships. In other words, we can get quite good at lying to one another!

We do not have to lie to one another in order to get along. Relationships based upon deceit and half-truths do not exist on solid foundations. We are told that the Holy Spirit will help us to exist peacefully with one another:

> Always keep yourselves united in the Holy Spirit,
> and bind yourselves together with peace.
>
> Ephesians 4:3

If we follow the guidance of the Holy Spirit, we can build our interpersonal relationships on solid ground. Some examples of building blocks for truthful relationships are as follows:

Matt Stephen, Ed.D.

1. We can give honest, careful, thoughtful, constructive feedback to one another.

2. We can accept one another's differences (physical, intellectual, philosophical, emotional, and spiritual) and be open to new ideas and opinions.

3. We can protect one another from falsehoods and develop mutual trust.

4. We can exhibit unconditional love for others.

Paul tells us that if we build our relationships upon a firm foundation of truth, we will be rewarded through the creation of binding, peaceful, trusting relationships.

Dear Father,

Thank you for the honesty in our relationships. Help us to be honest and trusting with one another. Amen.

Go With It

It is ironic, but sometimes the greatest lessons are the ones that are the least planned. I remember one day when I exchanged places with a student in the classroom. He was a very difficult student to teach. He was always interrupting and wisecracking from his seat. I constantly had to redirect him back on-task. One day I had enough. After numerous interruptions, I asked him if he would like to teach the class. He laughed and said that he would. He got up and started clowning around as the teacher.

Then an idea hit me. I took his place in the audience and began wisecracking! I had the best time watching him squirm. The students thought it was hilarious. Everyone had a good time, and we all learned something from it. I think we all walked out of that room respecting one another's position a little more. I realize now that I must have appeared a bit nutty to the students, but I believe this episode made me a little more human to them.

Spontaneity is enjoying each moment for what it has to offer. We should make an effort to enjoy our journey in life even if it means deviating from the planned path. Sadly, even though we spend countless hours planning our lessons to the minutest details, it may be those special, spontaneous, "off-the-wall" moments that the students remember the most.

A song in the book of Habakkuk speaks to us about enjoying the journey:

> Yet will I rejoice in the Lord, I will be joyful in the God of my salvation. The Sovereign Lord is my

Matt Stephen, Ed.D.

strength! He will make me surefooted as a deer and bring me safely over the mountains.

Habakkuk 3:18–19

Joy can be planned or spontaneous. In the classroom, at home, or out in the world, we can rejoice in the Lord; and he will help us to walk on the clouds. We can enjoy every minute of our journey as we walk with the Lord.

Dear Father,

Please help us to be more spontaneous and enjoy each minute for what it has to offer. Help us to spread your joy to our children. Amen.

April

April is a busy month. It usually includes standardized testing, proms, banquets, sports tournaments, and field trips. Celebrations such as Keep America Beautiful Month, Mathematics Education Month, National Library Week, National Volunteer Week, Professional Secretaries' Week, Week of the Young Child, Take Our Daughters to Work Day, and National Arbor Day give us ideas for exciting activities for our students.

This month the last grading period begins, and we are facing our last chance to help students achieve success. We often feel extreme pressure at this point to get our students to meet state standards. Teamwork can pull our school through the fires of standardized testing. Districts need to remember that it is who we've got, not what we've got, that makes the difference. It is our teachers, not our materials or programs, who truly determine our students' success.

The month of April is packed with activities, yet it seems to pass by slowly. For many of us, this month begins the longest stretch of the year, from April Fool's Day to the last day of school. Unfortunately, the weather at this time of year is not cooperative. It can be quite rainy and overcast much of the time, and we find ourselves rarely getting outside. Our days are so much better when students can get outside and burn up some energy!

April can be a dangerous month for relationships. With the year ending too quickly and frustrations flaring all around us, we need to model and practice patience and empathy. Our fortitude is tested by many circumstances. We can ask God for his strength and protection and work with him on forgiving others as well as ourselves.

This can be the most challenging month for student discipline. It is a long stretch from Spring Break to the end of the year, and students get tired of constantly complying with rules. The best defense is a good offense. Numerous activities to keep everyone busy and interested in learning are the key to success. This calls for extensive planning up front, but it pays huge dividends. We can work together with colleagues to determine the most effective activities for our students' success.

Matt Stephen, Ed.D.

Standardized Tests/
Non-Standardized Children

One of the greatest frustrations for educators today is the loss of freedom in teaching due to standardized testing. We feel smothered by the expectations put upon us by outside forces, and often it is questionable whether these forces truly know what standards are best for children. In the classrooms, we can see the adverse results of too much pressure on children to succeed. We often force children to learn at a level that is too advanced or at a pace that is too rigorous. We force "non-standardized pegs" into "standardized holes." Imagine us physically pushing children to crawl through windows that are too tight for them to fit. It would be a painful ordeal for students and teachers alike. How close is this image to the reality of standardized assessments? Educators sometimes feel that they are expected to do the impossible at a terrible cost to the children.

We are under immense pressure to increase our students' performance on standardized tests. Perhaps we can better deal with standardized tests if we examine their purpose. Our legislators are in favor of educational standards and standardized assessments because they believe that the data from these assessments will prove to the taxpayers that schools are improving student learning. This is not a bad premise; however, educational standards and standardized assessments are not perfect because they are created by imperfect humans. As servant leaders, we are frustrated because we see the imperfections in the system, and we see the impact of the high-pressure testing on our students.

Standardized assessments aside, we should always pressure ourselves to increase our effectiveness in helping children learn. Curriculum or materials alone will not make the difference for our children. The greatest factor for student success is the personal relationship established between the child and the teacher. We know that we must stay informed and be flexible in our teaching. We are driven to do whatever it takes to ensure our students' success. We will follow our states' standards, and we will use whatever instructional strategies or materials we think work best for our students. If we keep our focus on the children and do what is best for them, we will continue to cover essential skills and have faith that the standardized tests will take care of themselves.

Paul tells us that each person receives unique gifts:

> Now there are different kinds of spiritual gifts, but it
> is the same Holy Spirit who is the source of them all.
> 1 Corinthians 12:4

Each of our students is a unique individual with special gifts from God. We can establish personal relationships with our children and learn about their gifts. If properly developed, these gifts can be used to God's glory. We can consider our children's gifts as we determine how to instruct them. Our children are not standardized; therefore, our approach to loving and teaching them should not be standardized.

Matt Stephen, Ed.D.

Dear Father,

Thank you for not standardizing us. We glory in our individuality. Help us to treat your children differently according to their needs and gifts. Amen.

Meditations

Katharine Hepburn once said in an interview that we should listen to the song of life. Could there be a more beautiful way to say, "Stop and smell the roses?" In the hustle and bustle of life, we often forget to do this. Think of the beautiful plants, animals, art, literature, and music that we sometimes miss because we are in a hurry! As followers of God, we are promised the ability to experience his Fruits of the Spirit (Galatians 5:22–23):

- Love,
- Joy,
- Peace,
- Patience,
- Kindness,
- Goodness,
- Faithfulness,
- Gentleness,
- and Self-control.

Unfortunately, we inhibit our ability to enjoy these blessings as we hurry through our rapid-paced lives. Think of a typical day at school. How many fruits of the spirit do we experience each day? If we are missing these blessings from God, how can we recapture them?

First, we can get out of our ruts by not always doing the same thing each day. We can look for new and fun activities to do. We can get in touch with the child in

Matt Stephen, Ed.D.

us and let go of our inhibitions. We can do something crazy and surprise everyone. Spontaneity and variety are the spices of life!

Second, we can focus on building positive relationships with the people around us. We can train ourselves to see the best in everyone. We can be aware of the good in people and spend less time contemplating the bad. Through these relationships, we can help our students build their best possible futures.

The last suggestion is the most important. We can slow down and find the time to meditate. This will involve rearranging or changing our priorities. God is always with us, but we do not hear him unless we are quiet. Through peaceful mediation, we can hear what he has to say. By allowing God to speak to us and guide us, we will see that through him we can overcome the world.

Paul gives us great advice about how to meditate:

> Fix your thoughts on what is true and honorable and right. Think about things that are pure and lovely and admirable. Think about things that are excellent and worthy of praise. Keep putting into practice all you learned from me and heard from me and saw me doing, and the God of peace will be with you.
>
> Philippians 4:8–9

We are promised God's peace if we will meditate on that which is good. The other fruits of the spirit will also follow. Through quiet purposeful meditation, we can make a conscious effort to slow down, count our blessings, and appreciate all that is good in life!

Dear Father,

Please help us keep our minds on you and your will. With your help, we can concentrate on the good in those around us—especially your children. Help us to dwell on the positive events in our lives and to leave the pitfalls in your hands. Amen.

The Language of the Hand

We use our hands to communicate with others throughout our lives. We use them to speak of love, dependence, independence, and interdependence.

When your years numbered two,
you said, "I need you.
Hold my hand. I am nervous. I need help. Watch me.
I need you to hold me close. Stay with me. Don't leave me."

When you were ten or so,
you told me to let go.
"Let go of my hand. I can do this alone. I am moving on. I don't need your help anymore, but stay close just in case."

At eighteen and grown,
you said you were ready to be on your own.
"Let go and stand back. I don't need your lectures. I don't need your rules. I don't need your restrictions."

When you were thirty or better
You said, "Let's get back together.
Hold my hand again. I need your advice. I need your experience. I need your strength."

In my final hours on this earth,
as I lay waiting for my rebirth,
you reached out for my hand and said, "I will miss you.
I need you to hold me close. Stay with me. Don't leave me."

Throughout life, we seem to go full circle about our need for help from others. As servant leaders, we are called to hold people's hands. Some people want us to remain close to them while others want to be more independent and distant. We are willing to support others at whatever level they seek. God tells us that he is always here to hold our hands:

> I am holding you by your right hand—I, the Lord your God. And I say to you, "Do not be afraid. I am here to help you."
>
> Isaiah 41:13

> The steps of the godly are directed by the Lord. He delights in every detail of their lives. Though they stumble, they will not fall, for the Lord holds them by the hand.
>
> Psalm 37:23

Through it all, God is here to hold our hands and offer guidance and protection. Likewise, as servant leaders, we are to take others by the hand and guide and protect them.

Dear Father,

Life is precious and short here on earth. Hold my hand as I hold the hands of your children. Amen.

Hide and Seek

Children have a game that they have played for generations called "Hide and Seek." There are many variations on the game, but essentially, it consists of one person seeking another until the other is found. The game can last a few seconds or several hours depending on the rules and the tenacity of the players. Think back to when you played the game. What was the thrill for you? Was it the process of seeking others and being surprised when you found them or was it the process of hiding and springing out at someone when they found you? Maybe it was showing off your prowess as you detected where the others hid or found perfect hiding spots that no one else could find.

We still play Hide and Seek every day as adults. More accurately, we play a game called "Seek." As educators, we constantly seek more knowledge and success. To better serve our students, we seek the best math systems, the best reading programs, the most effective instructional delivery models, the most effective classroom management model, or the most accurate diagnostic or evaluation tools. Being adverse to failure, we seek these answers with the same desperation that we showed when we searched for friends years ago in a game. Have you found all of the answers to your professional challenges: curriculum, instruction, discipline, assessment, and time management? Also, have you found all of the answers to the challenges in your personal life? If not, where do you go from here?

Jesus has an answer for us:

Keep on asking, and you will be given what you ask for. Keep on looking, and you will find. Keep on knocking, and the door will be opened. For everyone who asks, receives. Everyone who seeks, finds. And the door is opened to everyone who knocks.

Matthew 7:7–8

God does not hide the answers from us. He waits for us to seek his guidance. Too often, we depend only upon our own resources in searching for answers. On occasion, we will ask our colleagues, friends, or family members for help. Often, we wait until we have exhausted all possibilities before we, in frustration, go to God. Jesus tells us to seek our answers through God from the very beginning. It sure sounds like a time-saver!

Dear Father,

Please help us to remember that we are not alone. You have the answer we seek. Thank you for allowing us to come to you for solutions. Amen.

Matt Stephen, Ed.D.

Service with a Smile

Do you remember how the service industry once went out of its way to serve others? At a full-service gas station, the attendant filled the gas tank, checked the oil level, and cleaned the windshield before we drove away. If we got out of the car, it was only to pay a visit to a spotless restroom. Grocery stores, milk companies, and pharmacies made home deliveries, and doctors made house calls. Waitresses and counter personnel were friendly and talkative, and banks did not charge for conveniences. In fact, banks gave toasters and small appliances to customers who opened new accounts. Everyone smiled and was glad to be of service.

The service spirit in America is not totally dead—just severely wounded. There are a few companies who focus on customer relations and take pride in the level of service they provide. More often than not, we see few smiles from those in service positions. As customers, we often experience impersonal interactions, selfish attitudes, indifference, slow service, poor quality, and little follow-up from service personnel. Many times I, the customer, am the only one who says, "Thank you."

Why this change in service attitude? Our society has changed in ways which have caused some of our traditional services to become outdated. High-speed technology and communications have created a faster-paced society. Some people have developed a "me first" attitude which places everyone else a distant second. Our population has exploded, and mobility has dramatically increased. All of these changes make it more likely that there will be fewer personal interactions among people. As a result, many people and companies have developed a more impersonal service attitude.

Although times are different, Paul's advice about a service attitude is timeless:

> Work hard and cheerfully at whatever you do, as though you were working for the Lord rather than for people.
>
> Colossians 3:23

We are serving the Lord when we serve his children. Because we serve the Lord, we serve with gladness! As educators, we cannot afford to lose the "service with a smile" attitude. We must work toward more positive customer relations with our children and their parents. We can strive for the highest quality output and take joy in sharing these experiences with the children. We can personally ensure our students' success and well-being and know that we can make a difference. With a smile, we can guarantee to our customers that we care about them and their future!

We are given more advice to help our service attitudes:

> Love each other with genuine affection, and take delight in honoring each other.
>
> Romans 12:10

We can take an attitude of delight in honoring our customers. We can dedicate ourselves to delighting our students, their parents, and our communities.

Matt Stephen, Ed.D.

Dear Father,

We know that we are serving you when we serve your children. We promise to honor you as we cheerfully serve your children. Amen.

One Day at a Time

Have you noticed how little time educators tend to spend in the present? Campus and district planning processes have us constantly reviewing the past and looking to the future. There is tremendous value in reflecting on the successes and challenges of past efforts. Examining future goals and creating plans for action are critical for creating new directions to take to improve student achievement. However, with all of the time we spend learning from the past and looking ahead to the future, how much time do we really spend engaging in and enjoying the present?

If we do not feel we are spending enough time focusing on the present, we can examine what prevents us from enjoying the present. Regrets from the past can rob us from enjoying today. If we do not forgive the transgressions of the previous day and begin anew, we allow guilt to cloud our pleasure. Fear of the future can also take away the joy of the present. Dreading the events of tomorrow, next week, or next month can bury the joys of today.

Most of all, we tend to miss out on enjoying the present because we forget to slow down and appreciate every day events such as watching a bird in flight, listening to the wind, watching children at play, or smelling a flower. I have always believed that the function of the modern day poet is to slow down, observe life, get in touch with the human spirit, and report findings back to others. Perhaps each of us can get in touch with our "inner poet" and find ways to enjoy the present moments.

Missed opportunities are great tragedies. We must live for today because it is all we are guaranteed. We should

Matt Stephen, Ed.D.

be aware of God's beautiful earth. There is so much to observe and for which to be grateful.

We received some great advice from Jesus and King David about worrying:

> So don't worry about tomorrow, for tomorrow will bring its own worries. Today's trouble is enough for today.
>
> Matthew 6:34

> This is the day the Lord has made. We will rejoice and be glad in it.
>
> Psalm 118:24

Jesus tells us that if we spend today worrying about tomorrow, we double up our problems; and King David encouraged us to spend each day rejoicing over that day so there would be little time left for worry.

Dear Father,

Thank you for creating this beautiful world for us. Help us to slow down and take advantage of what this world has to offer each day that we are here. Amen.

Secretaries' and Paraprofessionals' Day

A special love poem to our secretaries and paraprofessionals who:

Can carry on multi-conversations and tasks
and answer questions before anyone asks.

Can please all staff, no matter how picky,
will clean up others' messes, no matter how icky.

Often accept the blame for what others do
and refuse compliments, regardless how few.

Are always willing to serve up dignity by the bowl-full,
even to those who are acting like a whole-fool!

Will take barbs and arrows meant for another
and hand out reminders better than one's mother.

Can pull us out of many a scrape
with only glue, eraser, scissors and tape.

Most of all we appreciate that loyal smile
that helps us postpone our troubles for awhile.

Because we are thankful for their presence each day,
we ask God for a special blessing to come their way.

All of us can tell stories of how we were once saved by a secretary or a paraprofessional. They are the unsung

Matt Stephen, Ed.D.

heroes of our schools. They are fiercely loyal, incredibly hard-working, positive climate builders, and great public relations agents. They are often over-worked, under-paid, under-appreciated, and taken for granted; yet, they continue to smile and support us each day.

Our secretaries and paraprofessionals are far ahead of most of us when it comes to sacrifice. Often they work for little more than minimum wage, and they shoulder much more of the burden than is required of them. They truly are following Christ's law:

> Share each other's troubles and problems, and in this way obey the law of Christ.
>
> Galatians 6:2

Dear Father,

Thank you for our loyal secretaries and paraprofessionals who shoulder our burdens every day. Help us to better show our appreciation for their support. Amen.

Dump the Mental Garbage

A garbage bin can get nauseatingly pungent after a couple of days if one misses the regular garbage pick-up. The garbage fouls the air and overwhelms our senses. This is exactly what happens if "mental garbage" lies around our brains for very long. It can begin to foul our minds and take over our positive thoughts. Mental garbage is made up of resentment, jealousy, revenge, pessimism, and other negative thoughts. These thoughts and emotions are dangerous because as they lie around and fester, they can pollute our minds and foul every aspect of our lives.

Rumor and gossip are vehicles in which this mental garbage can spread. Every workplace has its optimum breeding ground for this mental garbage to grow and do its damage. Where is this spot in your school? Is it the staff lounge, the office, cafeteria, the parking lot, the Internet? Is the rumor mill alive and well at your school? Are you a vital link in the gossip chain? God tells us through King Solomon that rumors and lies are very powerful weapons:

> Telling lies about others is as harmful as hitting them with an ax, wounding them with a sword, or shooting them with a sharp arrow.
>
> Proverbs 25:18

God tells us that lies and rumors are nothing short of deadly weapons! If we are carrying these weapons at school, we must dump them before they hurt someone and cause irreparable damage to our climate. Not only do we need to drop the weapons of gossip and rumors, we

Matt Stephen, Ed.D.

need to cleanse our minds of the smelly mental garbage that arms these weapons. Once we rid our minds of mental garbage, we are directed to replace it with kindness:

> Since God chose you to be the holy people whom he loves, you must clothe yourselves with tenderhearted mercy, kindness, humility, gentleness, and patience.
> Colossians 3:12

Dumping mental garbage is difficult because society tends to steer us toward negative thoughts. All one has to do is watch primetime television or read a newspaper to get the latest in pessimism and negativism. There is hope. We can learn to recognize negative thoughts and consciously rid ourselves of them. We can be aware that being positive requires a sustained, purposeful effort on our part. We must make a conscious effort every day to keep our thoughts positive.

It will help to find those people in our school who also avoid negative thoughts and converse with them daily. They will help by encouraging us to think and speak positively. By seeking out these positive people, we will avoid those who are mired in their own dark, self-defeating attitudes. The negative people will seek us out because they seek to add our company to their misery. We can disappoint them by being a role model of positive thinking. Perhaps through our model, they will see what a positive attitude can do for them.

Dear Father,

Help us to cleanse our minds of all mental garbage and refill them with your mercy and kindness. Please keep our minds focused on your love and inspire us to spread your positive message of life to others. Amen.

To Be or Not to Be

In the classroom, we are constantly "on stage" with our students. They watch us every minute of the day. We find ourselves acting out certain roles and putting on different faces for different situations. We develop many different personalities: one for the classroom, one with professional colleagues, one for the boss, one with friends, one for home, one for church, and one for the community. We can sometimes get lost in our different roles, and we have to ask ourselves, "Which one is the real me?"

It is easy to confuse roles in different situations. We find ourselves correcting children's behavior in supermarkets, movie theaters, or sports events (much to the dismay of their mothers). We find ourselves straightening books or cans in stores. We might correct a friend's grammar or spelling. There may be some occasions where we say, "I hope none of my school kids are around" when we are being our public selves. We have all confused our different roles at times, and it can be quite embarrassing!

It is important not to get too confused and lose our "real" selves in all the different roles that we play because we model our values and character for our children every day. We need to ensure that all of our roles reflect our "real" selves - the character that God would have us model for his children. As Paul tells us:

> Be an example to all believers in what you teach,
> in the way you live, in your love, your faith, and
> your purity.
>
> 1 Timothy 4:12

We are to establish an ideal pattern for our children to follow. We are told to "walk our talk." Not only are we to have high expectations for the students' behavior, we are to exhibit an exemplary character to the students on a daily basis. What we portray "on stage" at school as well as in other areas of our lives should be the role that God expects us to exhibit. It is too dangerous to live by more than one moral code because we will eventually confuse our roles and send our children the wrong message. God tells us to live by only one set of standards, his code of conduct!

Character education programs require educators to teach citizenship and moral character to the children. We can no longer concentrate strictly on academics. Our nation's moral fiber is continuing to unravel, and the public schools are charged with reweaving our moral tapestry. We need to be sure that we are modeling and teaching the character traits that will put our nation back on the right track.

Dear Father,

We will strive to live our lives by your standards. Help us to be the ideal for our students and to model your code of conduct at all times. By training your children in your will, we will strengthen our nation's morality. Amen.

Matt Stephen, Ed.D.

Life's Adventures

Isn't it refreshing to know that life is full of adventure? We never really know what is around the next corner. Will our next experience be a major or minor event? Will it be depressing or exhilarating? Will it help us grow or tear us down? Each day holds the potential for ecstasy or disaster. When we wake up, we do not know which one it might be. Perhaps we cannot control what happens to us, but we can control how situations affect us. We can look at each experience, good or bad, as something from which to learn and grow. All adventures have a purpose—to mold us and make us who we are.

Often our first reaction after a bad experience is to say, "Wow! I want to forget this ever happened." This evasive action will not help us grow and learn from the experience. Reflecting after each experience is important because it allows us to think about what happened and draw conclusions from the experience. This is how we can turn a negative incident into a valuable one.

For example, I learned how not to teach from one of my undergraduate university professors. He was a negative, cynical, hateful man who did not enjoy the company of his students. Each hour with him lasted an eternity and was a test of my fortitude. I decided to study his mannerisms to ensure that I would never exhibit those traits as a teacher. I learned a lot about how to treat others through reflecting on his bad example.

We learn from everything that happens to us—success as well as failure. Next time something adverse happens to us, we can reflect on it until we receive some form of value from it. We need to be patient because it might take some time. There is something of value to be learned daily from every experience.

Paul tells us that our outlook on life is dependent upon our inner-selves:

> Everything is pure to those whose hearts are pure. But nothing is pure to those who are corrupt and unbelieving, because their minds and consciences are defiled.
>
> Titus 1:15

Our outlook on life determines how we are affected by what happens to us. We can see an experience either as destructive or as an opportunity for growth. We can either quit or become more determined to succeed. Think of the people you know who always see the good in every situation. Now think of the people who always see the negative side of things. Who is happier? Which outlook do we usually choose to take? God will help us to be pure of heart. He will help us look for the good in everything.

Dear Father,

Please help us to see the good in everything that happens to us. Enable us to learn from all of our experiences and maintain our purity of heart. Amen.

May

May is a month for celebration. We celebrate graduations, promotions, academic accomplishments, and end-of-year activities. "Moving forward" seems to be the motto for this month. The National PTA Teacher Appreciation Week and National Family Week give us reasons to celebrate important people in our lives.

This month takes on a hectic pace; however, the anticipation of the beginning of summer seems to dilute most of the stress. There is light at the end of the tunnel, and that helps us make it to the end of the school year. In spite of the hectic pace, we can slow down and savor the moments we have with our colleagues and students because some of these people will soon be moving out of our lives. Ending some of our relationships can be painful, so we can ask God to help us slow down and enjoy each moment with students, colleagues, friends, and family.

Beautiful spring weather and flowers lend an air of beauty and freshness to this season. We can be thankful to God for our lives and loves here on earth. Meditation on God and his glory can help us to appreciate our fleeting moments here in this life and look forward to our eternal life with God in Heaven. At the end of this month, Memorial Day gives us an opportunity to appreciate the people who have made supreme self-sacrifices so we can live in freedom.

Matt Stephen, Ed.D.

Team Spirit

One weekend I decided to quit school administration and become a softball coach. Not really, but I did get quite "fired-up" over what I witnessed at a school district's wellness softball tournament. My school staff fielded a softball team for the competition, and they gifted me with one of the most incredible team experiences I have ever witnessed. All individual players mixed together to create a team that surpassed all of our expectations and drove us to win first place in a tournament filled with fierce competition. Let me describe for you some of the team dynamics that enabled us to get to the top.

Our team played six games over a thirteen-hour period of fun, yet intense competition. Everyone shared a focus and sense of purpose. The coaches never had to stop and remind the players why they were there. Everyone was dedicated to the goal of winning first place. There was an air of mutual admiration and respect. All players had different abilities and talents, but they shared the same competitive spirit. The competition that occurred was not between team members, it was a shared competition against their opponents. The players supported one another through the good times and the bad; there was no gossip or backbiting. Our players were courageous; they made daring moves for the sake of the team, yet they were cautious when the situation called for it. We cheered one another's accomplishments and offered constructive criticism when needed. Our players showed disappointment when they did not execute their best; and instead of making excuses, they maintained an attitude of determination not to repeat mistakes. Our team demonstrated unrelenting endurance to accomplish the goal of first place by continuing to give it their all even after many hours of play!

When it was over, we knew we had accomplished a very special goal. The exhilaration was incredible! My thought later was, "It is too bad that we do not experience this exhilaration all of the time in other areas of our lives." Team competitions are short and intense. We cannot possibly sustain this level of competitive intensity throughout our daily personal and professional lives; however, we can remember these team spirit experiences and attempt to incorporate these actions into our daily routines as often as possible. At our schools, we can exhibit this same team spirit as we lead our children to their successes.

Paul gives us some specific ideas about team spirit:

> Love never gives up, never loses faith, is always hopeful, and endures through every circumstance.
> 1 Corinthians 13:7

Paul tells us that if we love one another, we will be loyal to one another, defend one another, believe in one another, and always expect the best from one another. If we are to work together as a team, we must be fiercely loyal toward one another. This means putting others ahead of ourselves. Our colleagues and our children come first. Together through team spirit, we can accomplish more than we dare to dream.

Dear Father,

So often, we try to do everything by ourselves. Please help us to rely more upon you and the others around us to accomplish our goals. Help us to keep a team spirit. Amen.

Are You Famous?

"Mr. Stephen, are you famous?" These words floated up to me from the innocent little face of a child whose hand I was shaking. As the newly appointed elementary school assistant principal, I was walking the halls of my school, shaking hands and introducing myself to the students. I was feeling quite "pumped-up" and important at the time. Taken aback by the question, I had to think for a moment. Yes, I was quite important here at this school, but hardly famous. So my answer to the child was, "Well, I suppose I am pretty important here at this school, but I am not famous." The more I think of this response, the less I think of it.

As educators, are we famous? I think so. By definition, famous means having a widespread reputation, renowned, and celebrated. Only a handful of educators achieve national or international acclaim. Their deeds and accomplishments are highlighted and celebrated. Those of us who do not achieve this status still make a difference in our own communities. Perhaps millions of people do not know or admire us, but I daresay we touch thousands of lives over the spans of our careers. As each year passes, more students fall under our guidance and leadership. Our students' parents and siblings also witness our character and actions. As a result, our influence becomes more and more widespread.

It seems tragic to me that many educators say to themselves and to others, "I am only a teacher." What has happened to us? Teaching, once the noblest of professions, has lost its prestige. Because educators are not highly paid,

Matt Stephen, Ed.D.

highly publicized, or highly revered by the public, many believe that the profession has lost its importance. I disagree. Educators have the most important and challenging function in our society—to improve children's lives and shape the future of our world. What other profession or vocation can be more crucial than this?

Be assured that educators are highly renowned and celebrated by God. He knows our trials and joys. He follows each of our lives day by day. He is aware of our every move. He has even numbered the hairs on our heads (Matthew 10:30). We may not be famous celebrities here on earth, but when the time is right, God will see to our reward.

The time we spend here on earth is not to be used for storing up earthly treasures and striving for human accolades. There is much more valuable work to be done. As Jesus said:

> Don't store up treasures here on earth, where they can be eaten by moths and get rusty, and where thieves break in and steal. Store your treasures in heaven, where they will never become moth-eaten or rusty and where they will be safe from thieves. Wherever your treasure is, there your heart and thoughts will also be.
>
> Matthew 6:19–21

Even though society sometimes chooses to look down upon the teaching profession as ineffective and upon educators as second-class professionals, our reward is in God's hands; and his hands are the ones that make all the difference!

Dear Father,

Thank you for the opportunity we have to shape our children's lives. It is an awesome task to shape tomorrow's world, but with your help, we can do it. Guide us as we humbly serve your children. Amen.

Matt Stephen, Ed.D.

Stirring the Nest

After a baby eagle (eaglet) hatches, it is totally dependent on its mother. The mother eagle feeds it, cleans it, keeps it warm, and protects it from predators and the elements. The eaglet would probably stay in the nest forever if not for the mother's natural instinct to "stir the nest." When it is time for the eaglet to leave, the mother eagle stirs the nest so that sticks will prick the eaglet and make it uncomfortable. With the comfort level gone, the eaglet grows restless and wants to spread its wings and fly away.

> Like an eagle that rouses her chicks and hovers over her young, so he spread his wings to take them in and carried them aloft on his pinions.
>
> Deuteronomy 32:11–12

As leaders of children in our schools, we can get very comfortable with where we are at the moment. We can even become complacent and not want things to change. I believe that God "stirs our nests" to keep us moving forward. He changes our environment and causes us to become restless. This stirring of the nest may be in the form of an overbearing boss, a dislike for co-workers, unhappy parents, disapproval of campus or district policies, a discontent with the job itself, or just a deep desire to move on with one's career.

We must be willing to read the signs and be open to moving forward. God may be nudging us to change grade levels or schools, go back to college for another certification, or even change our entire vocation. Change can be painful and scary. The good news is that we are never alone. God stays with us. We must remember that God will carry us after he stirs our nests and our discontent. We can be willing to move forward with confidence that God will support us. As we spread our wings and make that leap of faith toward the unfamiliar, we must be open to the directions that God will lead us and continuously seek his will.

Dear Father,

Thank you for giving me a purpose in life as a leader. Help me not to be complacent and to embrace changes as they occur. Please direct me to where you want me to serve others. Amen.

Matt Stephen, Ed.D.

Silly Smiles

What I like best about watching the Summer Olympics are the "silly smiles" on the faces of the medalists. As they stand on the gold, silver, and bronze podia to receive their medals, they seem to be about to explode with happiness and fulfillment. It shows on their faces and in their smiles—the kind of smiles that they cannot wipe off their faces. Have you ever been so happy that you just could not help but smile? You were so happy that you thought your heart would burst or your face would crack from that huge grin. You tried to wipe that grin off your face, but you just could not do it!

We might surmise that "silly smile" episodes do not occur often at work. However, some people are paid to perform the same activity they would do free anyway, and they wear those smiles constantly. How fortunate they are! The reality is that most of us diligently work for our pay and the silly smiles come later during our off-duty hours. I wonder if it has to be that way—especially in our line of work. Can we generate activities and successes for our children that will give us enough happiness and fulfillment to experience those silly smiles? What can we do to ensure silly smiles for our students? In addition, what can we do to ensure silly smiles for our colleagues and ourselves?

Paul makes it clear to us how we should feel every day:

Always be full of joy in the Lord. I say it again—rejoice!
Philippians 4:4

God tells us to wear joy on our faces all of the time. He tells us to wear those silly smiles! So how can we ensure these silly smiles? We need to strive for those feelings of exhilaration where we feel so close to God that our bodies tingle. These fleeting moments are a sample of how heaven will feel. If our hearts are about to explode with the joy of God, how can we keep from smiling?

Dear Father,

Thank you for those moments that give us those silly smiles. Help us to multiply those moments and experience them more each day. We will share these moments with your children and our colleagues. Amen.

Matt Stephen, Ed.D.

Take a Number Please

It is possible to restrict our ability to serve our customers by strictly adhering to policies and procedures. Here is an example:

At the Municipal Court Building in a city where I once lived, I went to pay a traffic citation (for a friend, of course!). Upon entering the empty reception area, I walked up to the counter, caught the eye of one of the two receptionists, and explained my mission. She asked, "Did you take a number?" Baffled, I told her that I had not done so. She pointed and said, "Take a number please. Someone will be with you shortly." I walked over to the area where she pointed and found a ticket dispenser with a sign that instructed all visitors to take a number and sit down. I took the number twenty and sat down. I had ample choice of seats because all of the seats were empty. After about two minutes of appropriate paper shuffling, the woman said, "Sir, I can help you now." I thought about asking her to call my number, but I decided not to push my luck (I know that I have seen this before somewhere in a comedy routine on television).

As she processed the payment, I found myself leaning with both elbows on the counter. I then noticed that next to my right elbow was a sign, which had been taped to the counter that read: "Please do not lean on or bend over the counter." I snapped to attention and nervously waited for her to finish. At this point, I just wanted to get out of there before I broke any other rules. I was extremely uncomfortable, and I hoped that I would never have to return to that place!

I can't help but wonder if there are any rules or regulations at our schools that we adhere to just for the sake of following rules. If so, this is not a customer-friendly habit. Perhaps from now on when faced with a situation where a rule doesn't seem to fit, we will seriously question the validity of that rule. We should ask ourselves, "Does this rule help us to best serve our customers?"

Paul tells us how to serve others:

> For you have been called to live in freedom—not freedom to satisfy your sinful nature, but freedom to serve one another in love.
>
> Galatians 5:13

We are told that we have freedom only within the boundaries of loving and serving one another. Our guideline from God is to serve one another with love. When serving others out of love, we must be flexible and consider the individual circumstances of each situation. This will prevent us from possibly damaging relationships through strict adherence to rules and regulations that really do not matter anyway.

Dear Father,

Help us to consider the needs of people over the need to follow rules and regulations. Remind us that your children are our first priority. Amen.

Matt Stephen, Ed.D.

Mother's Day

Mother
Why do I love you?
Let me count the ways:

One–   because you make my life lots of fun
Two–   because you love me no matter what I do
Three–   because you chauffeur me all over the county
Four–   because you take care of my every hurt and sore
Five–   because you make me feel important and glad to be alive
Six–   because you put up with my silly tricks
Seven–   because you teach me about God, Jesus, and heaven
Eight–   because you make me eat everything on my plate (Not!)
Nine–   because you always look so fine
Ten–   because you give me hugs and kisses again and again

Happy Mother's Day!

As we honor our mothers on this Mother's Day holiday, let's remember what God told us thousands of years ago:

> Honor your father and mother. Then you will live a long, full life in the land the Lord your God will give you.
>
> Exodus 20:12

Mothers are perhaps the greatest of God's earthly gifts. Their clear demonstrations of unconditional love are models for us as educators. Like mothers, we love our students regardless of what they say and do. We are to "mother" our students as we model God's love.

Dear Father,

Thank you for mothers. Help us to learn from their loving examples. We promise to mother your children and teach them of your love. Amen.

Moving Up

When moving up in the world the old adage often rings true: "It's not what you know, it's who you know." Often, this is very true. I can think of many examples which illustrated that someone moved up or was recognized due to personal connections rather than superior knowledge, ability, natural talent, or hard work. This can be very frustrating. I am not sure anyone has figured out a fair and accurate way to recognize the best educators through a meaningful compensatory or advancement system. Many times it is those who get in good with the system who are recognized or rewarded whether they deserve it or not. Although we sometimes find this frustrating, it is a fact.

Working to get into someone's good graces can be a very good thing. Paul verifies that it is who you know that makes the difference:

> For I can do everything with the help of Christ who gives me the strength I need.
>
> Philippians 4:13

There is no doubt that a personal relationship with Christ will allow us to do all things—even moving up in the professional world. In addition, in moving up in the spiritual world, it is not what one knows, but who one knows that leads to success. Not all of the knowledge, skills, or personal connections in the world will gain us admittance into eternal life in heaven. Only a personal relationship with God and Jesus will accomplish that.

Even though we do not deserve the heavenly reward that we receive, we still move up based upon whom we know!

Dear Father,

We thank you for our relationships with you and your son, Jesus. We know that relationships with our fellow man will help us move up in this world, but our relationships with you lead to earthly and eternal rewards. Help us to concentrate more on heavenly rewards than earthly ones. Amen.

Serve Whole-Heartedly

Who cares if we work hard? Who notices that we spend late nights preparing lessons or grading papers? Who notices that we spend long afternoons at the media center or many hours decorating our rooms? Who notices when we deliver an outstanding lesson or finally get that elusive concept across to our students? We all look for those "Atta-Boys" or "Atta-Girls." In reality, there are very few accolades out there for us because of our hard work. And to top it all, there are people out there who do a lot less work than we do, and they seem to be reaping the same benefits. So why work hard? Why put in the extra time and effort?

Paul tells us that we should work hard for a very good reason:

> Work hard, but not just to please your masters when they are watching. As slaves of Christ, do the will of God with all your heart. Work with enthusiasm, as though you were working for the Lord rather than for people. Remember that the Lord will reward each one of us for the good we do, whether we are slaves or free.
>
> Ephesians 6:6–8

We are told that we should gladly work hard all of the time because we are working for the Lord. He promises us rewards for each good thing we do. God tells us that if we serve, we should serve well; and not to please others, but to please him. We are to work hard because we serve God with all of our heart. Being noticed by our employers in this life is nice. It is gratifying to have someone recognize our hard work and professional attitudes. However, our hearts and minds should belong to God. He is the one for whom we are working to please.

So who benefits from our hard work? Our children do! They are rewarded many times over because of our efforts. The children reap what we sow. This is the entire purpose of the serving spirit—others benefit from our work. Our benefits are God's peace here on earth and eternal life in heaven.

Dear Father,

Thank you for the reward of a good life here on earth and the eternal reward in heaven. Thank you for blessing us with a service spirit. Help us to persevere with our service spirit for the benefit of your children. Amen.

Your Symphony

If you have not seen the movie *Mr. Holland's Opus*, I suggest that you see it right away. It is about a music teacher who begins his teaching career with an "8–4" attitude. He reluctantly accepts a high school teaching position because he needs money to pay bills while he pursues his true passion of composing music. Through the years, he learns that teaching is more than imparting knowledge; it is also about giving the students a "compass" so they know how to use that knowledge. He realizes that his true calling is to provide direction for each individual student. At the end of the movie, he finds himself in an auditorium surrounded by his past and present students. He is exalted for his dedication to his students and to his profession. He realizes that the symphony he has worked on for thirty-plus years is not only musical notes on paper, but also the lives of the students that he has touched.

Paul tells us the way to keep perfect harmony in our lives:

> And the most important piece of clothing you must wear is love. Love is what binds us all together in perfect harmony.
>
> Colossians 3:14

Chances are we will not be able to gather all of our past and present students in one room at the end of our career. I wish we could because every educator deserves to go out in a flourish of love and adoration as Mr. Holland did. When we do leave the profession, what kind of symphony will people be playing about us? I hope it will be a symphony of love, adoration, respect, and appreciation. We know that there is much more to the education profession than most people realize. As servant leaders, we are truly here to lead children, not just to impart knowledge. So let's have fun with our children and continue to show them the right path. We can be their compass for direction, and one day they will collectively be our symphony.

Dear Father,

We realize that we are creating a symphony of lives as we mold your children according to your will. Help us to love all children so that they will sing your praises. Amen.

June

June is a month for reflections and farewells. We say goodbye to our students and to our colleagues for a while. We also reflect on our students' growth and our own accomplishments for the year. We wrap-up the school year in many ways: final grades and paper work (our writer's cramps will attest to that), evaluation of classroom and campus goals, evaluation of personal goals, prepare our rooms for the summer, and begin planning for next year. Along with the ending of another school year, Flag Day and Father's Day give us reasons to celebrate. Summer officially begins this month.

Summer is a time for self and family. No longer "on-call" and with no planning or grading during our off-hours, we give our families and ourselves some much needed attention. We rest, relax, and rejuvenate as well as play hard during our summer vacation.

We can take time this summer to celebrate our profession. We are doing God's work as we raise his children within his will. God has placed us in the perfect position to change the future for many people. We are making our mark on earth by improving the quality of life for the next generation. We are making our mark in heaven by adding more souls to spend eternity with God. I know God is pleased with us. We can talk to him and ask for his strength and guidance as we continue our efforts to serve his children.

Final Prayer

You are especially blessed because you have selflessly devoted your life to serving God's children. God is always with you. He will give you the strength, wisdom, and peace that you need to ensure that his children grow within his will. Call upon him whenever you need his counsel or his comfort. He is waiting.

> May the Lord bless you and protect you.
> May the Lord smile on you and be gracious to you.
> May the Lord show you his favor and give you his peace.
>
> Numbers 6:24–26

Dear Father,

We are grateful for the opportunity to serve you and your children. It is not an easy task, but we persevere out of love for you and your children. We continue to pray daily for your guidance to enable us to lead your children within your will, and we look forward to our eternal reward with you. Amen.

listen|imagine|view|experience

AUDIO BOOK DOWNLOAD INCLUDED WITH THIS BOOK!

In your hands you hold a complete digital entertainment package. Besides purchasing the paper version of this book, this book includes a free download of the audio version of this book. Simply use the code listed below when visiting our website. Once downloaded to your computer, you can listen to the book through your computer's speakers, burn it to an audio CD or save the file to your portable music device (such as Apple's popular iPod) and listen on the go!

How to get your free audio book digital download:

1. Visit www.tatepublishing.com and click on the e|LIVE logo on the home page.
2. Enter the following coupon code:
   1d6d-5524-04e8-c597-5f5c-4138-36b2-806e
3. Download the audio book from your e|LIVE digital locker and begin enjoying your new digital entertainment package today!